→INTRODUCING

ROUSSEAU

DAVE ROBINSON & OSCAR ZARATE

This edition published in
the UK and the USA
in 2011 by Icon Books Ltd,
Omnibus Business Centre,
39–41 North Road, London N7 9DP
email: info@iconbooks.com
www.introducingbooks.com

Sold in the UK, Europe and Asia
by Faber & Faber Ltd,
Bloomsbury House,
74–77 Great Russell Street,
London WC1B 3DA or their agents

Distributed in South Africa
by Jonathan Ball,
Office B4, The District,
41 Sir Lowry Road,
Woodstock 7925

Distributed in Australia and
New Zealand by
Allen & Unwin Pty Ltd,
PO Box 8500,
83 Alexander Street,
Crows Nest, NSW 2065

Distributed in the USA
by Publishers Group West,
1700 Fourth Street,
Berkeley, CA 94710

Distributed in Canada
by Publishers Group Canada,
76 Stafford Street, Unit 300
Toronto,
Ontario M6J 2S1

ISBN: 978-184831-212-8

Originating editor: Richard Appignanesi

Printed and bound in the UK by Clays Ltd, St Ives plc

I Myself, the Unique ...

Jean-Jacques Rousseau changed forever the ways in which we think of ourselves, both as individuals and as members of society. He warned us of the dangers of our modern civilized world and anticipated its imminent collapse. In spite of all this, he remained an optimistic writer and a man who always knew that he was absolutely unique.

Childhood in General

Jean-Jacques Rousseau was born on 28 June 1712 in Geneva. His mother died of puerperal fever shortly after his birth. His father, Isaac, was an unstable and very quarrelsome watchmaker who kept getting into trouble with the authorities. He had been to Constantinople for six years as watchmaker to the Sultan's harem.

Rousseau also had an elder brother, François, who ran away to Germany and was never heard of again.

Isaac encouraged his son to read the classics, especially Plutarch's **Lives,** and to be a patriotic citizen of Geneva, a small Calvinist republic surrounded by large Catholic states. Rousseau was mostly self-educated, which meant that he was not always very widely read or self-critical.

I ADMIRED THE CITY-STATE OF SPARTA AS PLUTARCH DESCRIBED IT, BECAUSE SPARTANS WERE COURAGEOUS IN WAR AND HAD FIRM EGALITARIAN AND COLLECTIVIST VIEWS.

But Rousseau's relationship with his own city-state was more ambivalent.

Restricted Freedom

Geneva was strictly Protestant and ruled over by 1,500 of its most important citizens. (The whole population was about 20,000.)

ITS LEGISLATIVE BODY, THE GENERAL COUNCIL, COMPRISES ALL THE ELIGIBLE CITIZENS.

ITS AUTHORITARIAN GOVERNMENT, THE PETIT COUNCIL, MAKES ALL THE DAY-TO-DAY DECISIONS ABOUT THE PUBLIC AND PRIVATE LIVES OF GENEVANS.

AS AN INDEPENDENTLY MINDED YOUNGSTER, I SOON RESENTED ANY RESTRICTIONS PLACED ON MY OWN PERSONAL FREEDOM.

Rousseau eventually fled the city for more liberally minded company. Nevertheless, even though he spent most of his life as an exile, he usually referred to himself as "a citizen of Geneva".

Early Adventures

Rousseau was boarded with a local pastor in Bossey, a village near Geneva, where he was unjustly beaten for stealing a comb. He was also chastized by the pastor's sister, an experience he rather enjoyed. When he was fourteen, he was apprenticed to an engraver, Abel Ducommun.

HE FREQUENTLY WHIPPED ME FOR READING LIBRARY BOOKS WHEN I SHOULD HAVE BEEN LEARNING HOW TO ENGRAVE.

On 14 March 1728, Rousseau returned late from a walk to find himself locked out of the city, so he decided to escape. He was quickly "rescued" by the priest at nearby Confignon, who then sent him to **Madame de Warens**, a woman famous for converting runaway Protestant youths to the Catholic faith.

Madame de Warens

Mme de Warens was probably the most important influence on Rousseau's life. She was beautiful, clever, eccentric and a rather dubious character who had run away from her husband to Savoy. She lived on a pension from the King of Sardinia who employed her as a spy. She had a house in Annecy and was an intrepid entrepreneur, although few of her many schemes actually made any money.

While in Italy, Rousseau supported himself by becoming a rather haughty and unreliable servant to different aristocratic families. He already rather fancied himself as an intellectual and resented being treated as an inferior. In June 1729, he left Turin and returned to Annecy and the maternal bosom of Mme de Warens. It was a reciprocal arrangement.

She sent him to the Annecy seminary to become a priest, but he soon left to study music instead, at the cathedral.

The Traveller

Rousseau then spent several months travelling – to Lyons, Fribourg, Lausanne, Vevey, Neuchatel and elsewhere, having miscellaneous adventures in the company of various eccentric and dubious companions, all of whom he later described in his **Confessions**. He spent much of his early adolescent life on the road, travelling from town to town and fortunately seems to have been a charismatic young man, because he rarely found himself going hungry or having to sleeping rough.

He went to Paris for a brief time, but was soon back on the road again, and finally returned to the arms of Mme de Warens who, by now, had moved to Chambéry. For a short time Rousseau worked as a clerk, then taught music to the local young ladies – one of whom tried to seduce him.

11

Rousseau's Psychology

Rousseau was an unusual young man, the victim of many irreconcilable psychological tensions and sexual anxieties. He had an overwhelming need for a mother figure to give him a sense of security and welcomed the idea of female domination: "Oh to be at the feet of an imperious mistress, to obey her commands and ask her forgiveness …" All of this made his eventual relationship with Mme de Warens very disturbing.

From an early age he seems to have had a taste for sexual masochism.

Throughout his life he worshipped young aristocratic women and had naive, chaste fantasies about them, mostly based on his early reading of sentimental romances.

Les Charmettes

Mme de Warens eventually rented a small house, Les Charmettes, where Rousseau spent several idyllic years determinedly educating himself and leading the simple life.

It was probably at this time that the self-educated young scholar read political philosophers like **Samuel Pufendorf** (1632-94), **Hugo Grotius** (1583-1645), and the English philosophers **Thomas Hobbes** (1588-1679) and **John Locke** (1632-1704).

The End of the Affair

Rousseau persuaded himself that he had some kind of heart disease and went off to Montpelier to be cured. On the journey there he had another sexual adventure. He was seduced by a fellow traveller, Mme de Larnage. But, on his return, he found that the idyll of Les Charmettes was over.

By this time he was also writing songs, and had completed a short opera called **Narcisse**. He lacked the patience for young students, so his teaching job was not a great success.

Trying His Luck in Paris

After a short and unhappy return to Chambéry, Rousseau finally went to Paris to see if his unique system of musical notation could make his fortune. He presented it to the Académie des Sciences but, unfortunately, they were unimpressed.

> IT RELIES ON NUMBERS AND DOTS, WHICH MAKES IT SHORTER AND NEATER THAN THE MORE USUAL OVAL SHAPES ON STAVES.

> BUT IT'S MUCH HARDER TO READ AND NOT THAT ORIGINAL.

Nevertheless, his time wasn't wasted. Rousseau was an efficient "networker". In Paris he soon made influential friends like the philosophers **Etienne de Condillac** (1715-80), and the famous **Denis Diderot** (1713-84).

He also met Mme Dupin, a famous society hostess, and eventually accepted the position of secretary to the French ambassador in Venice.

HE DIDN'T GET ON WITH THE AMBASSADOR WHO TREATED HIM AS A SERVANT RATHER THAN AS A COLLEAGUE.

In Venice, he went to the Italian opera and made a disastrously embarrassing visit to a courtesan – Zulietta – who advised him to "leave the girls alone and study mathematics instead". He finally quarrelled with the ambassador and so returned to France.

Thérèse and the Children

In Paris, Rousseau stayed at the Hôtel Saint-Quentin. While there he seduced one of the servants, an illiterate country girl called **Thérèse Levasseur** from Orleans who became his life-long companion. She bore him five children. Rousseau sent every one of them to the foundling hospital. Bizarrely, he seems to have believed that this was in their own interest.

Although he invented several other ingenious and unconvincing excuses for his unnatural behaviour, Rousseau eventually admitted that he could never forgive himself for abandoning them, a feeling that his readers usually share.

The *"Philosophes"* and the Enlightenment

The intellectual friends that Rousseau met in Paris were known as the *"Philosophes"*, although they were more like social critics than true philosophers. They were reformers who wanted to improve existing society, rather than activists with a revolutionary programme. They were all key members of what is called the French "Enlightenment" – a cultural phenomenon that was well established by the middle of the eighteenth century.

SOME *PHILOSOPHES* WERE ATHEISTS AND MATERIALISTS WHO BELIEVED THAT RATIONALISM AND SCIENCE WOULD EVENTUALLY REPLACE ALL RELIGIOUS SUPERSTITION.

Others, like Rousseau, were Deists or lapsed Catholics. **Voltaire** (1694-1778) was a Royalist, **Montesquieu** (1689-1755), a parliamentarian, and others were Republicans. What they all shared was a scientific world view and an optimism about the future.

The Risks of Philosophizing

The *Philosophes* welcomed technological progress and the accompanying spread of commerce and industry across Europe. They insisted that human beings should use reason both to understand the world, and to modernize government and the law. They were against all forms of oppression and censorship, and believed in freedom of thought and expression. Many of the ideas popularized by the *Philosophes* derived from the English pioneers of Empiricism, like **Francis Bacon** (1561-1626) and John Locke. But the French *Philosophes* had to be more courageous than their English colleagues.

Diderot finally ended up in the dungeon of Château de Vincennes for his unorthodox views.

His new friend Rousseau regularly went on foot from Paris to Vincennes to see him, where he met other intellectuals like **Friedrich Grimm** and **Baron d'Holbach**. By 1746, Rousseau had become an important figure in the intellectual life of the French capital.

I AGREED TO CONTRIBUTE ARTICLES ON MUSIC AND POLITICAL ECONOMY TO THE GREAT *ENCYCLOPÉDIE* PRODUCED BY DIDEROT.

Rousseau was quickly adopted as a colleague, even though his ideas on most things were still half-formed. But then, on one of his walks to see his imprisoned friend Diderot, Rousseau had a "vision" which turned this obscure middle-aged musician into a world-famous philosopher.

Rousseau's Vision

In 1749, on the way to Vincennes, Rousseau had seen a newspaper advertising a competition proposed by the Academy of Dijon. Competitors had to write an essay with the title "Has the rebirth of the sciences and arts contributed to the improvement or corruption of manners?"

THE INSTANT I READ IT, I SAW ANOTHER UNIVERSE AND I BECAME ANOTHER MAN ...

MERCURE DE FRANCE

HAS THE REBIRTH OF THE SCIENCES AND ARTS CONTRIBUTED TO THE IMPROVEMENT OR CORRUPTION OF MANNERS?

"Suddenly I felt my mind dazzled by a thousand flashes of enlightenment ... I felt overcome by a giddiness resembling intoxification ... I sank down under a tree in the avenue and there spent half an hour in such a state of agitation, that, on getting up, I saw the whole front of my jacket wet with my tears ..."

Rousseau arrived at Vincennes in a highly excited state of mind. Diderot, always a lover of controversy, told Rousseau that he must compete for the prize.

Civilization and Modern Man

The visionary revelation that had struck Rousseau so forcefully was the realization that men were essentially good, so it had to be all the institutions of modern civilization that had made them wicked.

CIVILIZATION AND PROGRESS HAS NOT MADE HUMAN BEINGS MORALLY BETTER OR HAPPIER. AND, IN THE END, CIVILIZATION WILL DESTROY EVERYTHING THAT WILL TRULY MAKE US HUMAN.

IT WAS A STARTLING AND UNORTHODOX VIEW, WHICH ROUSSEAU STUCK TO FOR THE REST OF HIS LIFE.

AND IT MADE HIS CONTEMPORARIES EXTREMELY UNEASY.

Philosophers like Diderot and Voltaire were deeply committed to the progressivist "Enlightenment" and the benefits of civilization. If human beings would only allow themselves to be guided by reason then they would enjoy material, political and moral progress, and so become happy. Rousseau disagreed.

The First Discourse

Rousseau's philosophy nearly always emerges from his own personal experiences. As a simple and honest Genevan citizen, he had been shocked by the luxury and depravity of the Parisian aristocratic world which he had experienced on the margins as a servant and tutor. His own contribution to the Arts (his musical notation system) had recently been rejected. He was very conscious of his own poverty and general lack of recognition. His essay is partly a revenge on all those sophisticated Parisians who had "patronized" him (in both senses).

The **Discourse on the Sciences and the Arts** is an impressive rhetorical exercise, full of contradictions and paradox. Rousseau quickly admitted that it was badly written and inadequately argued.

The Falsehood of Civilization

In his essay Rousseau insists that civilized people are wearers of masks. Reality is always replaced by appearance. "Man no longer dares to appear what he is." Cultured individuals appear superficially polite and charming, but underneath they are full of fear, suspicion, hatred, treachery and cynicism.

THEY ARE LIKE PUPPETS CONTROLLED BY A RIGID CONFORMITY TO SOCIAL CUSTOM.

WE ARE ONLY WHAT OTHERS **EXPECT** US TO BE.

THIS HYPOCRISY MEANS THAT CORRUPTION AND IMMORALITY FLOURISH, AND BOTH PRODUCE POLITICAL AND MILITARY DECAY.

Modern men are made weak and selfish, enslaved by material possessions and alienated from their true selves.

What Good Are Luxury and the Arts?

Civilization also encourages a love of luxury which reinforces inequality. The role of the Arts and Sciences is merely to disguise injustice and "fling garlands of flowers over the chains". It is also wrong to further social inequality by awarding distinctions to a few superior artists or scientists (even to those who win essay competitions, presumably).

ROUSSEAU CONCLUDES BY INSISTING THAT A STUDY OF HISTORY SHOWS ALL OF THIS TO BE TRUE.

GREAT EMPIRES ARE ALWAYS DEFEATED BY MORE PRIMITIVE AND VIGOROUS CULTURES WHICH HAVE WISELY REJECTED THE ARTS AND SCIENCES.

The Spartans practised self-denial, truthfulness, military prowess and patriotism, and so beat the more cultured Athenians in war.

Inconsistencies and Criticisms

Most of Rousseau's contemporaries thought that his essay was little more than a rather laboured attempt to argue an implausible case merely for the sake of controversy. Rousseau's essay also seemed uncertain about whether the Arts and Sciences were a primary cause or just a secondary effect of decadence. Others pointed out the all too obvious inadequacies and inconsistencies of Rousseau's historical "evidence".

And finally, if these reactionary views about past "Golden Ages" were true, why did men abandon them for something worse? Did Rousseau want to burn all the libraries, close the universities, and return Frenchmen to a state of ignorant and lawless barbarism?

Fame at Last

Whatever its flaws, **The First Discourse** made Rousseau famous overnight, perhaps because of its shock value, perhaps because it appealed to the deep, but normally unspoken suspicions people have always had about the human enterprise called "civilization". By now Rousseau was relatively successful. He was secretary and cashier to the influential Dupin family, met with the famous intellectuals of the day, and ate with his wife's rather less glamorous family in the evenings.

THERE WERE SIGNS THAT HE WAS BECOMING CONVINCED BY HIS OWN "SYSTEM".

I RETIRED AS SECRETARY TO THE DUPINS, DRESSED VERY SOMBRELY, WORE A PLAIN WIG AND BECAME DETERMINED TO PURSUE A LESS COMPLICATED EXISTENCE.

This didn't stop him from writing the opera **The Village Soothsayer**, performed for King Louis XV at Fontainebleau. It was very successful and suggests that Rousseau could have become a famous composer had he wanted to.

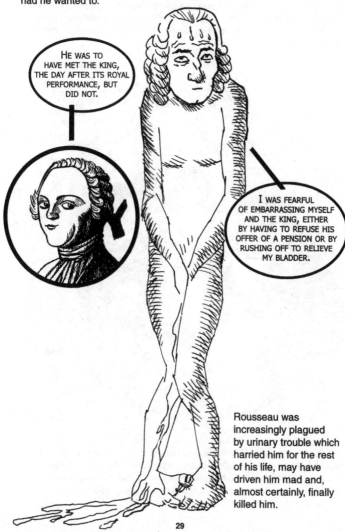

HE WAS TO HAVE MET THE KING, THE DAY AFTER ITS ROYAL PERFORMANCE, BUT DID NOT.

I WAS FEARFUL OF EMBARRASSING MYSELF AND THE KING, EITHER BY HAVING TO REFUSE HIS OFFER OF A PENSION OR BY RUSHING OFF TO RELIEVE MY BLADDER.

Rousseau was increasingly plagued by urinary trouble which harried him for the rest of his life, may have driven him mad and, almost certainly, finally killed him.

Rousseau's Theory of Language

In Venice, Rousseau had begun an essay on **The Origins of Language**, in which he claimed that, like everything else that was human in origin, modern language was corrupt because it had departed from its original purposes. The first men communicated their physical needs with wholly transparent gestures and signs, which made them incapable of lying.

THE MOST ENERGETIC LANGUAGE IS THE ONE IN WHICH THE SIGN HAS SAID EVERYTHING BEFORE WE SPEAK.

THEIR FEELINGS AND EMOTIONS WERE EXPRESSED IN SONG-LIKE PHRASES, IN A LANGUAGE WHOLLY METAPHORICAL.

The most appealing languages originated in the south, where the climate was mild, the land fertile and the living easy, which is why they sound soft and melodic. Life and language were harsher in the north. Modern languages eventually became shrill, dominated by grammatical rules and the need for precision. Prose and its demand for the literal conquered the immediacy of song.

Writing then tied language down even further and made it the servant of abstraction and speculation. The complexity of modern languages is not a sign of progress but of degeneration. Modern language was invented to lie and deceive.

Derrida's Deconstruction of Rousseau

Rousseau saw clearly that language determines the possibilities of thought for all civilized peoples. The problem of "language and truth" has been persistent ever since Plato. Does language "mirror" truth? That is the inescapable conclusion Rousseau tries to avoid and, to do so, he slips from one excuse to another. **Jacques Derrida** (b. 1930) calls these excuses "supplements" that pile up in Rousseau's text and can be **deconstructed**.

Rousseau had tried unsuccessfully to determine whether language or society came first. The question is unanswerable. Using language to investigate itself will only result in an inconclusive tangle. But Rousseau was moving on to consider how "natural" it was for humans to live in societies. And that was the subject of his next discourse.

Another Competition

In 1754, The Dijon Academy announced another prize essay title: "What is the origin of inequality among men and is it authorized by natural law?" The implication of the title is that the social inequalities of rank and class are no more than inevitable offshoots of *natural* inequalities, like height and strength. It was an argument that infuriated Rousseau.

ALL THE REST OF THE DAY, I BURIED MYSELF IN THE FOREST ... I CRIED ALOUD TO THEM WITH A FEEBLE VOICE THEY COULD NOT HEAR: "MADMEN WHO COMPLAIN UNCEASINGLY OF NATURE, LEARN THAT ALL YOUR ILLS COME FROM YOURSELVES."

The **Second Discourse** marks Rousseau out as a true philosopher rather than a mere "essayist". It is sometimes difficult to follow because Rousseau kidnaps words like "natural" and "freedom" and assigns his own meanings to them. It can also be puzzling because it is a series of arguments with other political philosophers like Grotius, Locke and Hobbes.

What Is Human Nature?

A hypothesis about human nature is usually an unavoidable part of any political theory. Societies are made of human beings, so it seems sensible enough to start by investigating the material they are made of. But even early Greek philosophers like **Protagoras** (490- 420 BC) quickly realized that human societies are immensely varied.

THIS IMPLIES THAT THERE PROBABLY ISN'T ONE STABLE OR CONSISTENT "HUMAN NATURE".

HUMANS ARE "ESSENTIALLY" SOCIAL BEINGS, AND SO FUNCTION AT THEIR BEST AND HAPPIEST WHEN GOOD CITIZENS.

FOR US, MEN ARE SELFISH AND WILL ALWAYS BEHAVE BADLY UNLESS RESTRAINED BY LAW AND STRONG POLITICAL INSTITUTIONS.

"MODERN" HISTORIANS AND PHILOSOPHERS LIKE MACHIAVELLI (1469-1527) AND HOBBES DISAGREE.

MEN AGREE TO SUBMIT TO THE ABSOLUTE AUTHORITY OF GOVERNMENTS BUT ONLY BECAUSE THEY NEED PROTECTION FROM EACH OTHER.

ARISTOTLE (384-322 BC)

Rousseau's Version

Rousseau's theory of human nature is different from these "essentialist" doctrines. For him, "human nature" is so unique that it is probably a mistake to think about "human nature" at all. Human beings have a history. They have changed from one state (as isolated, simple and "innocent" primates) to another (the complex, civilized and social beings that we are now).

Rousseau saw that human beings are immensely malleable. There are only human **natures**. His view of the continuous flexibility of human nature and its relationship with the social and cultural world is one that had a huge influence on the political philosophies of **G.W.F. Hegel** (1770-1831) and **Karl Marx** (1818-83).

The State of Nature

If all societies are different, this also suggests they are artificial and not "natural" at all. It also suggests that pre-social or "natural" human beings had once existed in a "state of nature" long before societies or politics got invented. This idea of a "state of nature" is frequently used by political philosophers to describe a pre-political world. For Hobbes, the "state of nature" is always one of war and an ever-present threat.

WHEN GOVERNMENTS CEASE TO EXIST, THE CHAOS AND VIOLENCE THAT FOLLOWS IS HORRIBLE FOR EVERYONE.

LIFE SOON BECOMES "SOLITARY, POOR, NASTY, BRUTISH AND SHORT". LOCKE IS LESS PESSIMISTIC.

THE STATE OF NATURE CONSISTS OF MEN OF PROPERTY ALMOST CIVILIZED ALREADY, ALBEIT WITHOUT CLEARLY DEFINED PROPERTY RIGHTS OR CIVIC DUTIES.

Rousseau's own "state of nature" is a much more subtle and complex state of existence, more anthropological and remote in time. It was also mostly theoretical and fictional.

Laws of Nature

The competition essay title also referred to "natural law". So what is that? Political philosophers like Grotius and Pufendorf insisted that there were universal "natural laws" that are always true and valid, regardless of society's laws. "Natural" laws are derived from human nature.

IF YOU BELIEVE THAT MEN ARE RATIONAL AND SOCIABLE BEINGS, THEN YOU CAN DERIVE "NATURAL LAWS" FROM THESE QUALITIES WHICH PROMOTE SOCIABILITY AND MINIMIZE DISUNITY.

BUT THE VERY OBVIOUS PROBLEMS WITH "NATURAL LAWS" ARE THAT THEY ARE INEVITABLY GENERAL AND VAGUE, CANNOT BE MADE COMPULSORY AND RELY ON A PRESCRIPTIVE ACCOUNT OF HUMAN NATURE THAT NOT EVERYONE AGREES WITH.

IT MAY BE JUST AS "NATURAL" FOR US TO BE RUTHLESS AND COMPETITIVE, AS HOBBES SUGGESTS.

THE SECOND DISCOURSE
J. J. ROUSSEAU

Rousseau himself wisely avoids any talk about "natural law" because he is highly sceptical about some kind of permanent or essential "human nature".

Nature and Natural

All of this brings us up against the probably unanswerable question of what the word "natural" actually means. Unfortunately, words like "nature" and "natural" just don't have any "real" meaning. For Aristotle, the word "natural" meant "that which is essential to something", and not accidental or artificial.

Sometimes he gives it the more recent meaning of "the countryside" or, more profoundly, "the ordered universe that is created and designed by God". But at other times its meaning seems wholly subjective and signifies merely "that of which Rousseau approves".

Natural Humans

According to Rousseau, man's original nature was "good", but has since been corrupted by artificial society. This means that inside each modern man lies the vestiges of an earlier, better self. But it is impossible to describe what original "natural men" were like. All Rousseau has to go on is modern man. But modern man is like the statue of Glaucus, dragged from the ocean depths.

This is why Rousseau makes it clear that he cannot tell us historical truths about "natural men" but only invent suppositions which aid his philosophical enquiry.

"It is no light enterprise to disentangle what is original from what is artificial in the actual nature of man and to know well a state **which no longer exists, which perhaps never existed and will probably never exist ...** The researches that can be undertaken concerning this subject must not be taken for historical truths, but only for hypothetical and conditional reasonings better suited to clarify the nature of things than to show their true origin."

So, rather alarmingly, Rousseau says ...

I WILL DISCARD ALL THE FACTS, BECAUSE THEY DO NOT BEAR ON THE QUESTION.

Noble Savages and Orang-utans

There was some empirical evidence around to suggest what "natural men" might once have been like. Rousseau was well aware of the existence of contemporary nomadic hunter-gatherers elsewhere in the world. He knew about the great apes, which many eighteenth-century philosophers thought were a kind of "early man". Rousseau even anticipated evolutionary theory by proposing that distinct species might be related in some way and that the boundaries between species were less "fixed" than supposed.

HE ALSO SUGGESTED, IRONICALLY, THAT IF ORANG-UTANS WERE INDEED A KIND OF "SPEECHLESS SAVAGE" ...

... THEY ONLY REFUSE TO TALK BECAUSE THEY HAVE NO WISH TO BE ENSLAVED BY WHITE EUROPEANS.

Rousseau was very critical of Europeans and their conduct in Africa and the New World, and he abhorred the institution of slavery.

Apes and primitive men were often and misleadingly reported as innocents living harmonious lives of happy ignorance. This then led to the myth of the happy "noble savage" used by several eighteenth-century writers in order to mock modern civilized life. There was also much philosophical conjecture about the essential features of "human nature".

Unfortunately, human beings have probably evolved to be social language-users, so to raise a child in this cruel manner would merely produce something non-human and prove nothing.

Rousseau's State of Nature

Rousseau had his own firm views about pre-social natural men.
Hobbesian "natural men" were ruthless competitors. Rousseau's are more
like amiable chimpanzees, peacefully wandering around in the forest. They
are solitary beings without family, friends or property of any kind.

Ruled by the two sentiments of "self-love" and "pity", they are impelled
to preserve their own lives and have innate feelings of compassion.
They are few in number, non-competitive and self-sufficient, without
concepts of property, justice, industry or war. They are pre-moral beings.
Violence is always conceived of as merely an injury, not a "crime".
Natural men never experienced loss of esteem or suffered from feelings
of social inferiority. They were happier than we are now.

Natural Men and Hobbes

This idyllic picture of our ancestors really only tells us about Rousseau's own yearnings for a time of lost innocence. It is also, in part, a reaction against the "natural men" of Hobbes and Grotius. In **De Cive**, Hobbes stressed how an innate and unchanging lust for glory causes war among pre-social men. Rousseau thought it was wrong to think of "natural men" as being similar to modern men. His "natural" men are solitary beings who only meet occasionally. They rarely get the chance to compare themselves with others and so make no social or hierarchical distinctions. The only inequality between them is merely that of physical build and strength.

MEN, BY COMMON CONSENT, ARE BY NATURE AS EQUAL TO ONE ANOTHER AS ARE ANIMALS OF THE SAME SPECIES.

Socio-biologists would now be reluctant to accept this idealization of early man. Many animals, including human beings, seem to be naturally social and hierarchical. Chimpanzees live in stratified social groups, fight local wars and are occasionally cannibalistic.

Natural Men and Grotius

More optimistically, Grotius had suggested that primitive men were originally sociable and rational. What made them truly human was some form of association with each other. But Rousseau's lonely natural men have no language and so cannot form anything other than simple ideas based on immediate sensations. They are also "good" and "innocent" only in the passive sense of doing no active harm.

MEN IN THAT STATE HAVE NO KIND OF MORAL RELATIONSHIP NOR KNOWN DUTIES.

This makes them rather like animals, ignorant of morality and incapable of civilized behaviour involving logical thought or cooperation. So it's impossible to derive "natural laws" out of their "nature".

Modern Men

Having established what natural men were like, Rousseau goes on to describe the disastrous choices human beings then made in their journey from innocent goodness to corrupt civilization. As the climate changed and the population grew, human beings concentrated into tribes in order to hunt more successfully.

This meant that they began to notice each other, identified who their neighbours were, and comparisons then led to jealousy, inequality, vanity, envy and humiliation.

Modern Society

Rousseau concludes that there is nothing inevitable or "natural" about the institution of property or social inequality – both arrived because of deliberate choices made in the past. These decisions were then legitimized by social and political "contracts".

HUMAN BEINGS AGREED TO LIVE TOGETHER ACCORDING TO CERTAIN LAWS, BECAME OBSESSED BY THE CONTINUAL COMPETITION FOR RANK AND SOCIAL POSITION, AND CREATED AN UNEQUAL AND BRUTAL SOCIETY WHICH HAS PRODUCED MISERY FOR NEARLY EVERYBODY.

Human beings finally inflicted a coercive government on themselves whose sole function was, and still is, to protect wealthy property owners.

Contracts and Property

It is Rousseau's firm belief that property is the root cause of all social ills. "The first who enclosed a piece of ground and said 'This is mine' and found others simple enough to believe him, was the true founder of civilized society … Don't listen to this imposter; you are lost if you forget that the fruits of the earth belong to all and that the earth belongs to no one …"

Locke never thought to question the concept of "property" as such.

IN MY "STATE OF NATURE", MEN HAVE ALWAYS POSSESSED PROPERTY AND HAVE A "NATURAL" IF NOT A LEGAL RIGHT TO OWNERSHIP.

GOVERNMENTS ARE ONLY INVENTED TO SETTLE ARGUMENTS ABOUT PROPERTY CLAIMS.

LOCKE EVEN SUGGESTS THAT LIFE AND FREEDOM ARE KINDS OF "PROPERTY".

In Rousseau's state of nature, natural men initially had no understanding either of property or of "rights". But then a few greedy individuals who were cunning, articulate and persuasive suggested that everyone join in a "social contract" to ensure the rule of law, guaranteeing universal security.

The Chains of Property

By legitimizing and sanctifying property rights, the rich are then able to seize most of the land and pauperize the majority. Social relations become those of master and slave.

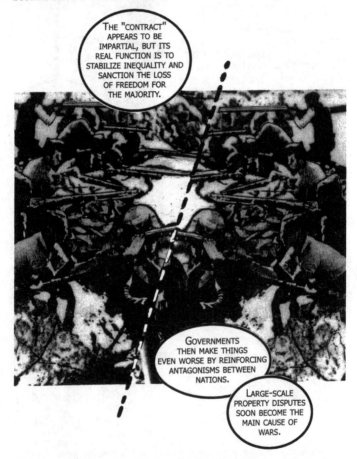

THE "CONTRACT" APPEARS TO BE IMPARTIAL, BUT ITS REAL FUNCTION IS TO STABILIZE INEQUALITY AND SANCTION THE LOSS OF FREEDOM FOR THE MAJORITY.

GOVERNMENTS THEN MAKE THINGS EVEN WORSE BY REINFORCING ANTAGONISMS BETWEEN NATIONS.

LARGE-SCALE PROPERTY DISPUTES SOON BECOME THE MAIN CAUSE OF WARS.

Rousseau agrees with the contractual explanation of how societies and governments began, but he argues that any such "contract" was always fraudulent and now has no binding effect on anyone.

Choosing Another Path

Because we are human, and therefore free, we have been able to change our natures for the worse. Inequality has become endemic, as have immoral values and artificial behaviour. But all is not lost, because we are indeed free. Unlike animals, human beings have the reflective capacity of self-awareness.

Human beings can examine their lives and seek to improve them, once they realize that modern society is a conspiracy to prevent them from achieving their true potential. So it is possible to undo all that has been done. Men can make themselves. There is nothing inevitable about modern civilization. It can and must be changed.

The Reaction of the *Philosophes*

This **Second Discourse** went against almost everything that the French Enlightenment said was good. Voltaire and Diderot were mostly optimistic about civilization and spent their lives fighting against the reactionary forces of superstition and intolerance.

The materialist and determinist views of the *Philosophes* did not answer to the inner emotional lives and spiritual yearnings of many people. Empirical and scientific investigations of human beings were not enough. Rousseau insisted that fundamental truths about human nature were only discoverable through intuition and reflection. Human feelings were as likely to be a source of truth as any cold abstract reasoning. A whole new ideology was being invented.

Rousseau's Refuge

Rousseau eventually had the **Second Discourse** printed and dedicated it to the city of Geneva. This time it didn't win any prizes, and was received with some hostility by most of the *Philosophes*. Voltaire read it and wrote to Rousseau: "Sir, I have received your new book, written against the human race, and I thank you … Never was so much intelligence used to make us stupid. While reading it, one longs to go on all fours."

In 1754 Rousseau renewed his Genevan citizenship. The authorities treated him generously, demanded no back taxes and didn't enquire too closely into his relationship with Thérèse. He paid a visit to Chambéry, only to find Mme. de Warens sad and impoverished.

EVENTUALLY, THE VERY RICH MME. D'EPINAY (A FRIEND OF MINE) OFFERED HIM A REFUGE ON HER ESTATE AT MONTMORENCY IN A LARGE COTTAGE CALLED THE HERMITAGE.

RATHER UNGRACIOUSLY, ROUSSEAU AGREED TO LIVE THERE …

PROVIDED I AM NOT EXPECTED TO BE GRATEFUL!

It was while here that he wrote his most famous works.

Rousseau stayed at the Hermitage for five years where he tried to recapture the happy times he'd had at Annecy. He spent his time walking in the woods and writing, avoided Paris, and so got the reputation of being a misanthropic recluse. Rousseau's behaviour and his opinions were beginning to puzzle and annoy his contemporaries. He soon quarrelled with Voltaire about God and the true nature of Providence. The great Lisbon earthquake of 1755 had disturbed many Christians. It occurred on All Saints Day when most people were in church, and it killed over 10,000 Portuguese citizens.

IT IS IMPOSSIBLE TO BELIEVE IN A COMPASSIONATE DEITY IF HE ALLOWED SUCH NATURAL DISASTERS TO OCCUR.

Rousseau's **Letter on Providence** argued that such disasters were essentially still man-made.

IF THE PORTUGUESE HAD ONLY LIVED A SIMPLER, MORE RUSTIC AND SCATTERED EXISTENCE, WITHOUT CITIES, EARTHQUAKES WOULD DO LITTLE REAL DAMAGE.

And in our hearts, we still recognize the existence of a benevolent divine plan. Human suffering is only a small part in the large and benevolent scheme of things (a view that Voltaire later satirized in his novel **Candide**, published in 1759). This was the real beginning of Rousseau's quarrels with nearly all of the *Philosophes*.

The First Romantic

Parisian intellectuals thought that Rousseau had chosen to live in a solipsistic fantasy world. And to some extent they were right. Rousseau was behaving as we now expect Romantic poets and artists to behave. On occasions, he was ecstatic with what his eighteenth-century friends would probably have called "enthusiasm" – a kind of intense and irrational religious insanity.

... THE EXCITEMENT OF MY RAPTURES MADE ME CRY OUT SOMETIMES: "O GREAT BEING! O GREAT BEING! UNABLE TO SAY OR THINK ANYTHING MORE ..."

In his imagination, Rousseau was busy creating a group of more sympathetic fictional characters with whom he could have agreeable private conversations. (Thérèse had soon become bored with the daily routine of long walks in the woods.) These were two beautiful female cousins (Julie and Claire) and a young male tutor (St Preux), a very obvious, if idealized, version of himself.

Sophie, a Real-Life Julie

In May 1757, Rousseau became almost convinced that one of his imaginary characters had arrived at The Hermitage in the form of Mme d'Épinay's sister, Sophie, the Comptesse d'Houdetot. She was twenty-seven, had abundant curly hair, was extremely confident and full of enthusiasms. Her husband was dull, but fortunately she had a lover called Saint-Lambert who wasn't. In spite of all of this male luggage, Rousseau fell in love with her almost immediately.

SHE CAME; I SAW HER; I WAS INTOXICATED WITH LOVE ...

I SAW MY JULIE IN MME D'HOUDETOT ... CLAD IN ALL THE PERFECTIONS WITH WHICH I HAD JUST ADORNED THE IDOL OF MY HEART.

It was probably the first and only time that Rousseau ever had a true romance. It inevitably ended in tears, quarrels and recriminations, mostly between Rousseau and Mme d'Epinay and her lover Grimm who both thought the middle-aged Rousseau was making an idiot of himself. But out of all of this sexual infatuation there came a novel which became an astonishing success throughout Europe – **La Nouvelle Héloïse** (published in 1761).

La Nouvelle Héloïse

The characters of Rousseau's novel live in an idealized pastoral dreamworld, occasionally intruded upon by the more brutal realities of economics and class. An impoverished young tutor, St Preux, falls in love with his rich young student, Julie. Their love is frustrated by her father.

St Preux goes into exile, but eventually returns and finally consummates the affair. Both parties threaten suicide – St Preux by jumping off a mountain.

The relationship ends when Julie marries the aristocratic Wolmar and afterwards thinks of the tutor only as the lover of her soul.

THE NOVEL STRESSES THAT WOMEN ARE DESIGNED BY NATURE TO BE VIRTUOUS WIVES AND MOTHERS AND NOT MISTRESSES.

St Preux returns from abroad to be the tutor of Julie's two boys and unsuccessfully attempts to restart the affair. The novel ends when Julie rescues her child from drowning but dies of pneumonia. Everyone is impressed with Julie's increasingly saintly demeanour.

It's a long novel, told in the then fashionable epistolary style, and full of many subplots and characters that are not very believable. Rousseau's theatrical characters are often rather obvious mouthpieces for his own views and obsessions.

A Romantic Bestseller

Like the many thousands of romantic and sentimental novels that have since followed, it is obsessive about the loss of the heroine's virtue. (We are eventually reassured that Julie recovers hers by means of her marriage and her devotion to motherhood.) Nowadays, the dazzling overnight success of **La Nouvelle Héloïse** is hard to understand. But thousands of ordinary eighteenth-century readers (especially female) flocked to buy and read about the adventures of the two lovers.

IT OFFERS SEXUAL IRREGULARITY UNDER THE GUISE OF MORAL INSTRUCTION.

UNLIKE MOST EIGHTEENTH-CENTURY NOVELS, IT IS FULL OF DEEPLY FELT EVOCATIONS OF RURAL LIFE.

IT CELEBRATES THE JOYS OF DOMESTIC CONTENTMENT.

ROUSSEAU HAS INVENTED A NEW KIND OF LYRICAL LANGUAGE TO DESCRIBE HIS CHARACTERS' FEELINGS AND GLORIFY THEIR NATURAL SURROUNDINGS.

Aesthetic tastes were being changed and the complex cultural phenomenon we now call "Romanticism" was taking shape.

The Moral Letters

Sophie tolerated Rousseau's often embarrassing and indiscreet behaviour towards her for some time. She finally abandoned their friendship and probably never read **The Moral Letters**, which he wrote for her. (They weren't published until 1861.) In these letters, he continued his attack on many of the Enlightenment beliefs held by his former friends.

CONTRARY TO POPULAR BELIEF, INTELLECTUAL ADVANCES ARE NOT THE SAME AS TRUE WISDOM.

ECONOMIC PROGRESS DOES NOT BRING HAPPINESS.

HUMAN BEINGS ARE MORE THAN JUST LUMPS OF THINKING MATTER PUSHED AROUND BY PREDICTABLE FORCES.

We have souls that reach up to the heavens and it is that fact that, in the end, makes us truly human. "Reason crawls, but the soul rises aloft." As individuals, we can only discover our true natures by rejecting our inauthentic social selves. Unsurprisingly, this entails withdrawing from crowds, and finding personal contentment in a simple and "natural" existence.

Letter to D'Alembert

For most of his life, Rousseau was a voluntary exile from his native Geneva. This probably made it easier for him to invest it with his own unique ideas. He was frequently jealous and vindictive about anyone he disliked who chose to live there, or even nearby, like Voltaire. In 1758 he read an article on Geneva written by the French philosopher and mathematician Jean le Rond d'Alembert for the famous **Encyclopédie**.

D'ALEMBERT'S ARTICLE ECHOES THE VIEWS OF VOLTAIRE WHO SAYS THAT THE CITY WOULD BECOME A MORE CIVILIZED PLACE IF A THEATRE WERE ALLOWED THERE.

FOR MANY YEARS, GENEVAN CITIZENS HAVE INSISTED THAT A PERMANENT THEATRE WOULD BE HIGHLY UNDESIRABLE.

ACTORS LEAD IMMORAL LIVES AND PUBLIC PERFORMANCES GENERALLY ENCOURAGE VICE IN THE YOUNG.

Rousseau's **Letter to D'Alembert** agreed with the Genevans' conclusion but got there with different arguments.

A Spartan View of Theatre

Rousseau was always proud of this essay in which he tried to make his Geneva into something like a modern day Sparta. In his view, theatres encourage audiences to forget their social obligations to the state. People sit in the dark as isolated individuals and lose their sense of identity as citizens. Contemporary writers are too sophisticated and their ideas superficial. Worse, playwrights like Molière flatter their audiences by encouraging prejudice and vanity, and by ridiculing virtue.

THE DECENT CITIZENS OF GENEVA WOULD BE SHOWN A PESSIMISTIC AND DISTORTED VIEW OF HUMAN BEINGS.

The theatre would be one more unnecessary luxury that would lead to yet more social inequality. Genevans would do best to emulate the Spartans and stick to healthy uplifting communal activities like physical games and public dances (where young Genevans would be carefully chaperoned).

Rousseau's Views on Art and Music

Rousseau always insisted that aesthetic theories and feelings should not be thought of in isolation from moral and political ideas. Good art can encourage an attitude of contemplation, just as the natural world can at certain times, if we are receptive enough.

WE NEED TO ENTER INTO A STATE OF MEDITATION IF WE ARE EVER TO GET A FEELING FOR THE HARMONY AND ORDER OF THE UNIVERSE. ON OCCASION, THE BEST ART CAN HELP TO GET US THERE.

Rousseau was a professional musician and composer, and copied music for a living for most of his life. He had some firm ideas about music. He thought that it was the most profound of all of man's artistic achievements because it was able to evoke complex moods and stimulate the emotions, more powerfully than any of the other arts.

In the **Letter on French Music** and in the **Dictionary of Music** Rousseau created a considerable amount of controversy because of his criticism of contemporary French music. He admired the Italian opera.

THAT'S BECAUSE ITALIAN IS A SOFT AND MELLIFLUOUS LANGUAGE WHICH MAKES IT SUITED TO MELODY.

ROUSSEAU IS AGAIN PRIVILEGING A "MELODIOUS" SOUTHERN LANGUAGE OVER A "HARSHER" NORTHERN ONE.

French composers like **Jean Philippe Rameau** (1683-1764) had to invent complex harmonies and elaborate orchestral ornamentation in order to disguise the coarse and clumsy sounds of the French language. But music was at its best when simple and expressed in song, not when it was over-embellished with artificial musical decoration.

Émile, an Educational Novel

Émile began as a dissertation on education but, because the illustrative examples all concentrated on one boy, it quickly became a didactic novel instead. Its central message is clear: "Everything is good when it springs from the hand of the Creator; everything degenerates when shaped by the hand of man …"

THIS TRUTH IS ESPECIALLY RELEVANT TO HUMAN BEINGS THEMSELVES BECAUSE …

… THERE IS NO ORIGINAL PERVERSITY IN THE HUMAN HEART.

But civilized society soon gets in the way. It produces corrupt, unhappy individuals. There can be only two solutions to this problem of acquired human wickedness: either you change present-day society utterly, or you raise an individual wholly outside of society. It is the latter solution that the novel proposes – an innocent child will be taught by a tutor in a walled garden that the world cannot reach.

A Psychology of Childhood

In the eighteenth century and before, aristocratic children were treated as apprentice adults, protected from fresh air and exercise, instructed formally and given harsh punishments for disobedience or irrational behaviour. The philosopher Locke envisaged education as a rather grim kind of "stamping in" process and **Émile** is partly a reply to Locke's **Some Thoughts Concerning Education** (published in 1693).

Émile is a revolutionary book because it more or less invented the whole concept of "childhood" by redefining it in psychological terms. Rousseau saw that there is much more to children than chronology and physiology.

And because each child is different, they should all be allowed to develop "naturally".

Émile's Education

Émile is from an affluent family who can afford to hire a private tutor. The extraordinary educational experiment then begins. From the start, Émile is cloistered from the world. He is allowed to play in the open air and develop naturally, stage by stage, in a carefully controlled environment. Initially, he lives in a world of *things* and experiences only *pain* and *pleasure*.

HE SOON LEARNS ALL THE UNAVOIDABLE TRUTHS IN THE ORDERED SYSTEM OF NATURE — THE GROUND HURTS WHEN YOU FALL OVER.

EVENTUALLY, HE BUILDS UP SIMPLE EXPERIENCES OF SENSATION INTO MORE COMPLEX ABSTRACT IDEAS.

BUT IN HIS EARLY YOUTH ÉMILE IS MOSTLY LEFT ALONE — IN A PROCESS OF "NEGATIVE EDUCATION".

HE LEARNS HOW TO WALK AND TALK ONLY WHEN HE IS READY TO DO SO, AND MAKES DISCOVERIES AT HIS OWN PACE.

EACH AGE, EACH STATE OF LIFE HAS ITS OWN PARTICULAR PERFECTION, THE KIND OF MATURITY SUITED TO IT.

There is no point in teaching a small child complex ideas or appealing to his "reason" before he is ready. This is why books are neglected for first hand experience. (The only book Émile is allowed to read is **Robinson Crusoe**, full of practical advice.) The tutor then gradually stimulates Émile's natural curiosity by discreetly inventing structured learning situations. Émile's whole world becomes a kind of all-inclusive classroom and laboratory in which he learns through discovery.

And when he is finally ready to grasp more complex, abstract ideas, he is given lessons in history, morality and religion.

69

Émile and Ethics

Émile cannot remain a simple and passively "good" child of nature forever. He must become an actively "virtuous" citizen of the world. Émile's natural feelings of "pity" have to be converted into imaginative empathy for others. As he evolves, he is able to listen more attentively to the promptings of his conscience – the infallible guide to moral conduct heard in "the silence of the passions". Only then can Émile finally become truly "virtuous".

HE MUST LEARN HOW TO RESIST FEELINGS OF SELF-INTEREST AND CHOOSE A HIGHER COMMUNAL GOOD.

BEING TRULY MORAL IS NOT INSTINCTIVE OR "NATURAL". IT INVOLVES AN INNER STRUGGLE AND MAKING SPECIFIC CHOICES – A TRIUMPH OVER ONE'S PASSIONS.

Because he is a rich young man, Émile also requires instruction in the obligations that the wealthy have towards the poor. (Rousseau was attracted to the idea of a benevolent aristocracy and frequently benefited from their patronage.)

Sophie and the "Fair Sex"

Émile is then at last introduced to the female sex – in the form of Sophie. He is encouraged to believe that sexual feelings must always be associated with the emotion of love and expressed solely within the sanctity of marriage. Sophie's own early education is similar to Émile's but denied his later academic pursuits. She is trained instead to perform domestic duties and encouraged to excel only in recreational activities.

THIS IS BECAUSE "WOMAN IS SPECIALLY MADE TO PLEASE MAN", WHICH MAKES HER INCAPABLE OF COMPLEX ABSTRACT THOUGHT.

IF UNNATURAL AND UNJUST DISTINCTIONS ARE MADE BETWEEN MEN AND WOMEN, THEN, AS WITH ALL POWER RELATIONS, BOTH PARTIES INEVITABLY GET CORRUPTED.

THE DOMINANT PARTY WILL CONFUSE POWER WITH TRUTH AND THE SUBORDINATE ONE DEVELOP CUNNING STRATEGIES FOR SELF-PRESERVATION.

Perhaps the only good thing to be said about this part of **Émile** is that it infuriated **Mary Wollstonecraft** (1759-97) and stimulated her to write **The Rights of Woman** as a reply.

A Successful Experiment?

Émile remains a fascinating book, full of contradictions and paradox. It isn't very likely that you could ever isolate a child from society in the way that Rousseau suggests. Émile still exists in a small unequal "society" of two which contains an adult who is already "corrupted". Rousseau tells us that Émile must first be "denatured" if he is ever to join society and become a virtuous and patriotic citizen.

SO HIS "NATURAL" SELF EVENTUALLY HAS TO BE SUPPRESSED AND CONTROLLED ...

THIS ALMOST SUGGESTS THAT MY UNIQUE EDUCATION HAS BEEN RATHER POINTLESS.

Rousseau never seems to have resolved this obvious paradox. He seems to have thought that even modern civilized men must somehow come to terms with their natural selves. If they did, then they could still be happy and fulfilled, even in a corrupt society, but probably only as independent "outsiders".

Progressive Educationalists

Rousseau's doctrine of the "natural innocence" of children is allied to his conception of "Natural men" who are free of all civilized evils. Children therefore require a special kind of education. Freedom and happiness in childhood are crucial because whatever is experienced then will determine adult behaviour. This means that negative behaviour is always *acquired* – the adult bully must inevitably have been bullied as a child. This idea of "childhood creativity" influenced many 19th-century Romantics, especially those who spearheaded "progressive education", like the Swiss social reformer **J.H. Pestalozzi** (1746-1827) and later **Maria Montessori** (1870-1952).

INSTRUCTION MUST KEEP PACE WITH THE NATURAL DEVELOPMENT OF THE CHILD.

TEACHING MUST BE "CHILD-CENTRED" AND NOT INSTITUTIONALLY STANDARDIZED TO MEASURE THE CHILD'S "OBJECTIVE PROGRESS".

The problem is that Rousseau's "system" remains immune from any possibility of children's bad behaviour.

Persecution for "Natural Religion"

Émile changed Rousseau's whole existence. He was persecuted by the authorities because of it, and it made him a nomadic exile for the rest of his life. It wasn't his radical ideas on child-centred education that infuriated them but the religious ideas expressed by "Le Vicaire Savoyard" at the end of the book.

The priest begins Émile's religious education by telling him that God must exist because, just as we will our own movements, so the whole universe is willed into being by a presiding Deity whose nature is unknown to us.

THIS EXPLAINS WHY THE LAWS OF NATURE ARE REGULAR AND PREDICTABLE.

THIS BEING ... WHICH MOVES THE UNIVERSE AND ORDERS ALL THINGS, I CALL GOD.

The Vicaire then explains his own "natural religion", which now seems harmless enough but in the 1760s was regarded as extremely heretical.

God places us in the world to be happy, and we are all potentially good. We are all equipped with a conscience, the "immortal and celestial voice" which guides us in our thoughts and deeds. (That doesn't prevent many of us exercising our free will in the wrong way. This is why evil is always a wholly human phenomenon.)

THE VICAIRE'S RELIGIOUS BELIEFS LEAVE LITTLE ROOM FOR ORGANIZED RELIGION.

HUMAN BEINGS ARE BORN GOOD AND NOT IN SIN. EACH INDIVIDUAL MUST COME TO GOD IN HIS OWN WAY. RELIGIOUS DOGMA DOES MORE HARM THAN GOOD.

It wasn't long before Rousseau's book was condemned by the Archbishop of Paris, burnt in the streets and a warrant issued for his arrest.

Rousseau the Mystic

Rousseau was always a man of intense religious convictions, something else that marked him apart from the other *Philosophes*. In his letters to several of them, he continually described the latest developments in his religious beliefs and feelings. And on his solitary walks, he responded to the beauty of nature primarily because it revealed the order and harmony of God's universe to him and filled him with a sense of wonder. He continued to believe that religious faith was crucial for human beings and he maintained a deep inner conviction that human beings must possess immortal souls.

The Social Contract

Rousseau was always deeply critical of contemporary political society whose main purpose seemed to be legitimizing inequality and preserving economic slavery for the majority. Rousseau's own response to this nightmare was to isolate himself from all centres of economic and political power. Nevertheless, in **Émile**, Rousseau had come to recognize that people still have to live in societies – a natural life in the woods is no longer an option.

I KNOW VERY WELL THAT AN ISOLATED INTELLECTUAL HERMIT LIKE ME WHO REJECTS MODERN SOCIETY IS ACTUALLY DOING SOMETHING RATHER ARTIFICIAL. NO ONE IS EVER REALLY "NATURAL" OR "FREE".

It seems almost impossible to raise "untainted" men, like Émile. If that is so, then the only other possibility is the total reform of political society, and that is precisely what Rousseau sets out to do next in **The Social Contract** (originally part of a larger but unfinished work called **Political Institutions**).

Societies and Rules

If different individuals wish to live together, they can only do so if they are restrained and governed by rules, customs, traditions and laws. If there are no rules, there can be no society. And rules on their own aren't enough. Someone or something must have the "sovereign" or absolute authority to be able to enforce them. But Rousseau believed that the reasons had to be very good if they were to persuade us to relinquish our natural freedom.

Asking Awkward Questions

Human beings rarely ask *why* they should obey political authority. Most people do what they are told because obedience to authority is something they inherit. Secular authority also often comes with divine credentials which makes political and religious commands more or less the same. That's why monarchs were very enthusiastic about their "Divine Right" to rule. But by the 17th century, philosophers started to ask awkward questions about political obligation.

This is Rousseau's first question in **The Social Contract**: *"Man is born free and everywhere he is in chains. How did this change occur? I do not know. What can make it legitimate? I believe I can answer this question."*

Obligations, Self-Interest and Contracts

Why obey governments at all? The simple answer is that governments will lock you up if you don't. But for Rousseau there was more to it than just "might" being "right". Some 17th and 18th century philosophers suggested that obeying governments was in most people's *self-interest*, because governments provide everyone with security.

OTHERS INSIST THAT OBEDIENCE TO GOVERNMENTS IS JUST A BASIC **MORAL DUTY** — IF YOU BELIEVE IN THINGS LIKE JUSTICE, FREEDOM AND EQUALITY BEFORE THE LAW.

AN EVEN MORE CONVINCING ARGUMENT IS THAT, IF HUMAN BEINGS ARE TO CONFORM TO THE LAW AND OBEY GOVERNMENTS, THEY MUST DO SO **VOLUNTARILY.**

THIS MEANS THAT POLITICAL AUTHORITY IS LEGITIMATE ONLY BECAUSE IT HAS THE CONSENT OF ITS SUBJECT CITIZENS.

People make an initial "contract" with each other to form a society and then another one that gives the government the right to rule over them.

Hobbes' and Locke's Views on the "Contract"

Political authority is made acceptable because it is somehow created by us by means of a "contract" between the government and its citizens. Hobbes had a deeply pessimistic view of human nature and a fear of civil war. This is why once the contract was signed, he insisted it gave absolute power to the sovereign.

This meant that governments had to govern constitutionally and every individual's consent to either contract could be withdrawn at any time (although Locke was never very clear about how this could be done).

Problems with the Contract

Not all philosophers accept the "contractual" explanation of obligation and legitimacy. It's hard to see how some original political "contract" is binding on subsequent generations, and there's absolutely no historical evidence of one. **David Hume** (1711-76) and Utilitarian philosophers like **Jeremy Bentham** (1748-1832) and **John Stuart Mill** (1806-73) argued that contractual explanations of how governments come into being aren't really relevant or helpful.

GOVERNMENTS ARE A GOOD IDEA ONLY BECAUSE THEY ARE USEFUL TO US.

GENERALLY SPEAKING, THEY PRODUCE MORE HAPPINESS THAN MISERY.

MARXISTS BELIEVE THAT THE INDIVIDUAL HAS NO CONTRACTUAL OBLIGATION TO ANY "BOURGEOIS" GOVERNMENT, BECAUSE THE STATE IS MERELY THE INSTRUMENT OF ONE SPECIFIC CLASS.

ANARCHISTS REJECT ALL AUTHORITY, ESPECIALLY THAT OF GOVERNMENTS, BECAUSE THEY USE COERCION, AND THE USE OF FORCE IS ITSELF A MORAL EVIL.

The Meaning of Sovereignty

In the 17th and 18th centuries, the term "sovereignty" was normally applied only to monarchs. Hobbes believed that men are willing to agree to a contract with the king, even if that makes them voluntary slaves.

And if the only reason we obey the law is because we are forced to, then we are under no **moral** obligation to do so. For Rousseau, "sovereignty" is more like a property of equality, and politics a branch of ethics.

Voluntary Association

"Those who wish to separate politics and morality will never understand anything of either."

CIVIL ASSOCIATION IS THE MOST VOLUNTARY ACT IN THE WORLD; SINCE EVERY INDIVIDUAL IS BORN FREE AND HIS OWN MASTER, NO ONE IS ABLE TO SUBJECT HIM WITHOUT HIS CONSENT.

The argument between Hobbes and Rousseau centres on the difference between "being obliged" or forced, and "being under an obligation" which implies that some kind of personal choice is involved. Rousseau's view is that citizens must obey the law because they feel that they *should*, not because someone else *forces* them to. The State must indeed be a voluntary association.

Rousseau's View of Laws

Earlier political theorists suggested that secular laws were compulsory because they derived authority from the word of God. Others claimed that a society's laws were mandatory because they were based on "natural law", which tries to make governments and laws natural phenomena. Rousseau thought that compulsory laws could only be made acceptable if the sovereignty that framed them was *democratic* – so the legislative authority had to be the people themselves.

HUMAN BEINGS ARE "THE PEOPLE" WHEN SEEN IN THE MASS, "CITIZENS" WHEN THEY VOTE IN LEGISLATIVE ASSEMBLIES, AND "SUBJECTS" WHEN THEY OBEY THE LAW.

WHEN, AS "SUBJECTS", WE OBEY SOCIETY'S LAWS, WE, "THE PEOPLE", ARE "REALLY" ONLY JUST OBEYING OURSELVES AS SOVEREIGN "CITIZENS".

Freedom and Obedience

If it is we ourselves who prescribe what the laws are, then we are still "free", but in a very different sense to when we were "naturally free". For citizens, "freedom" is synonymous with "obedience", because the laws they obey are those they have made for themselves. People are willing enough subjects of their **own** laws.

IN MY IDEAL LEGAL DEMOCRACY, EACH AND EVERY MEMBER OF SOCIETY WOULD BE INVOLVED IN **PASSING LAWS**, BECAUSE EACH INDIVIDUAL WOULD BE EXPECTED TO **OBEY** THEM.

IT ALSO MEANS THAT CITIZENS WOULD NOT BE ALLOWED TO NOMINATE REPRESENTATIVES TO DO THEIR THINKING AND VOTING FOR THEM.

And this insistence on a participatory and universal democracy means that his ideal citizens could only ever belong to a small city state or a sparsely populated island.

What Is the "Contract"?

If human beings decide of their own free will to join together in societies, then they also have to be prepared to abandon their "natural liberty" in exchange for a new and more rewarding "moral liberty" based on a voluntary acceptance of the law.

> THEY THEN CEASE TO BE PRIMITIVE INDIVIDUALS RULED BY INSTINCTIVE "GOODNESS", AND BECOME FREE AND "VIRTUOUS" CITIZENS INSTEAD.

> THIS IS HOW CIVIC "FREEDOM" CAN COME TO MEAN THE SAME AS "OBEDIENCE".

And it is this gradual process of progressing from primitive isolation to communal agreement that Rousseau means by the "social contract". How or when any "agreement" is made is never very clearly explained, and remains more of a theoretical fiction than historical fact.

Organic Process

Rousseau thinks that a form of understanding between everybody would gradually emerge through an organic process rather than by some legal transaction. So the legal term "contract" seems an unhelpful and inappropriate term.

ROUSSEAU IS RELUCTANT TO EXPLAIN HOW NATURAL MEN WOULD ACQUIRE THE INTELLIGENCE AND ORGANIZATIONAL SKILLS NEEDED TO AGREE TO A "CONTRACT".

NEVERTHELESS, I INSIST THAT MY ANIMAL-LIKE MEN DO EVENTUALLY COME TO RECOGNIZE THE AUTHORITY OF SOMETHING CALLED "THE GENERAL WILL", BECAUSE THEY ALL PERCEIVE THE BENEFITS OF AN OBEDIENCE TO IT.

What is The General Will?

"The General Will" is at the heart of Rousseau's political theory. It is probably easiest to understand "The General Will" by comparing it to the will of an individual. When, in law, a government body or a company makes a contractual agreement, then it is often convenient to imagine the organizations involved as fictional "corporate persons". To some extent, Rousseau envisages society as a whole in that way.

Collective Identity

Another way of understanding "The General Will" is to recognize the crucial distinction that Rousseau makes between the individual and the citizen. People may be born as individuals but are made into citizens.

CHILDREN IN MY IDEAL STATE WOULD BE EDUCATED FROM AN EARLY AGE INTO COMMUNITARIAN VALUES ...

UNTIL OUR LOYALTY TO THE COMMUNITY WOULD BE VIRTUALLY SECOND NATURE.

INDIVIDUAL CITIZENS WOULD DERIVE THEIR SENSE OF IDENTITY FROM THE COLLECTIVE.

They would have a love of country engraved in their hearts and a respect for "The General Will" in their innermost soul and so, again, function as almost one being. *"They love it with that exquisite sentiment which every man living in isolation has only for himself."*

Citizens of a Single Community

Rousseau thought that the citizens' obedience to prescribed moral laws would then be as unavoidable and "natural" as their "obedience" to physical laws, like the law of gravity. When children became adult citizens and voted in regular meetings of the legislative assembly, they would always vote conscientiously for the whole community and not out of personal interest. Each citizen would vote according to individual conscience and never as a group or on party lines.

EACH CITIZEN IS PERFECTLY INDEPENDENT OF ALL THE OTHERS AND EXCESSIVELY DEPENDENT ON THE STATE.

THIS LOYALTY PREVENTS ANY ONE GROUP FROM MANIPULATING THE DEMOCRATIC ASSEMBLY IN ITS OWN INTERESTS ...

... AND SEIZING POWER AT THE EXPENSE OF THE MAJORITY IN ORDER TO BEGIN YET ANOTHER CYCLE OF INEQUALITY.

All individual citizens would agree to pass the same laws, because what is in "the interest of all" would be unlikely to vary.

Obedience to Freedom

So all would obey, but no one individual or group would command. And this is how "The General Will" is made concrete – by becoming embodied in law.

Obedience to "The General Will" would convert them from "stupid and limited animals" into "intelligent beings".

The Will of All

If individuals at the legislative assembly meetings were to vote simply out of self-interest, then all that would result would be "the Will of All". "The General Will" is something purer, nobler, more patriotic and altruistic. If, however, on certain rare occasions, conscientious but differing opinions did arise, Rousseau believed they would inevitably cancel each other out.

"THE GENERAL WILL" WOULD STILL EMERGE AS A KIND OF AVERAGE.

HE IS, HOWEVER, VAGUE ABOUT THE STATISTICAL METHODS REQUIRED TO PRODUCE A RELIABLE RESULT.

People as Sovereign

Like other contractual theorists, Rousseau gets into trouble when he examines the kind of obligations that disaffected minorities or individuals have when they refuse to be bound to any kind of sovereignty, even that of "The General Will". Rousseau's doctrines of "moral freedom" and "The General Will" mean that all members of society have to agree to the same laws.

THERE CAN ONLY EVER BE **ONE** BODY OF LAW WHICH IS GENERAL AND UNIVERSAL.

THE SOVEREIGN PEOPLE HAVE UNLIMITED POWER AND THERE CAN BE NO OTHER SOURCE OF AUTHORITY.

ONCE THE PEOPLE HAVE DECIDED ON WHAT THE LAWS ARE, THESE LAWS ARE ALWAYS RIGHT SIMPLY BECAUSE THEY ALWAYS REFLECT "THE GENERAL WILL".

THE SUPREME POWER NEEDS NO GUARANTEES TOWARDS ITS SUBJECTS, BECAUSE IT IS IMPOSSIBLE FOR THE SOVEREIGN BODY TO HARM ITS MEMBERS.

Any disagreement would inevitably frustrate this legislative process and, worse, threaten the harmonious unity of society.

Forced to Be Free

And this is where the doctrine of "The General Will" begins to ring alarm bells, because any individual who does not accept its rulings is automatically mistaken and so must be "forced to be free". There are many different interpretations of what Rousseau meant by "The General Will" and even more of his chilling phrase "forced to be free". Rousseau liked rhetorical flourishes and paradoxes.

"FORCING" PEOPLE TO BE "FREE" SIMPLY MEANS THAT, IN ORDER TO MAXIMIZE THE FREEDOMS OF THE MAJORITY, CERTAIN ANTI-SOCIAL INDIVIDUALS WILL HAVE TO BE RESTRICTED BY FORCE.

BECAUSE, IN THE LONG RUN, THEY ARE THEMSELVES PART OF SOCIETY AND SO BENEFIT FROM THE VERY LAWS THEY REJECT OR HAVE BROKEN.

Misguided Behaviour

Such wayward citizens are misguided because they are temporarily unaware of what they "really" want. They are more likely to be "weak" than "bad", and would have to be forced to behave as conscientious citizens – which doesn't sound too bad, but a certain unease still remains. There are many ways of detecting **totalitarian** governments.

The Sovereign Body and Government

Hobbes believed that Sovereignty and Government were the same thing. Rousseau strongly disagreed. Only citizens can be the "sovereign" body that make laws by meeting regularly and voting in assemblies. Rousseau's "government" is subordinate to the legislative assembly, and is no more than a body of officials that administers the law. This insistence on a separation between the legislative body and the government suggests that Rousseau wasn't very keen on the idea of a "people's government".

MY SOVEREIGN PEOPLE ARE ALLOWED TO MEET AND PASS GENERAL LAWS WHICH ARE TO THE BENEFIT OF ALL.

BUT IT IS THE GOVERNMENT THAT APPLIES THESE LAWS TO INDIVIDUAL CASES AND CIRCUMSTANCES.

Government By Aristocrats

Rousseau's government would always be on a short contract and subject to review so that it could never accumulate too much power or usurp the legislative assembly. Rather surprisingly, Rousseau then suggested that the best form of government would be made up of aristocrats.

THE ARISTOCRACY HAVE SUFFICIENT LEISURE TIME IN WHICH TO CARRY OUT THEIR PUBLIC DUTIES.

MOST OF US ALSO HAVE INDEPENDENT INCOMES AND SO ARE MORE LIKELY TO BE CONSCIENTIOUS AND IMMUNE TO CORRUPTION.

A democratic government made up of the people themselves would also cause confusion to arise between the very different roles of the legislative body and the government. If they were ever to become the same, this would lead to corruption.

The Legislator

Rousseau realized that the transition from "natural" to "social" and "political" would be problematic in the first few years. How would recently "denatured" and inexperienced individuals know how to frame the fundamental laws of society? His solution is to invent a temporary but powerful "Legislator" whose job is to act as a kind of political catalyst.

As soon as the social and political conditions were right and citizens were acting appropriately, he would then quietly disappear.

Civil Religion: Deism

Rousseau is one of the few philosophers who was interested in the psychological as well as the political motives that bind a people together. People need to feel a sense of belonging to the State. Voting in assemblies isn't enough to ensure total devotion. "On Civil Religion" is the last section of **The Social Contract** – one that Rousseau rather regretted adding at the last minute and then unsuccessfully tried to suppress. He thought that the social contract between citizens needed some kind of minimal religious sanction.

I SUGGEST THAT EVERYONE WOULD HAVE TO DECLARE THEIR BELIEFS IN THE EXISTENCE OF A BENEVOLENT DEITY AND IN THE FACT OF A RETRIBUTIVE AFTERLIFE WHICH REWARDS THE GOOD AND PUNISHES THE WICKED.

This mild **Deism** would then become the official State religion. It would encourage individuals to believe that a violation of State laws would be sinful as well as illegal.

Against Christianity

Orthodox Christianity would be undesirable for several reasons. It places too much emphasis on the afterlife instead of on good citizenship, and a powerful Church would produce timid citizens with divided loyalties. *"True Christians are made to be slaves."* Rousseau's state would not make enquiries into the specific religious beliefs of any individual. It would only refuse to accept anyone as a citizen who was an atheist or a religious fanatic.

Rousseau the Realist

Although Rousseau's political philosophy might seem abstract and remote from everyday human affairs, in practice he was more of a realist. If a society already had a set of agreed customs, habits and laws that seemed to work well, and everyone agreed that they were acceptable, then these traditions could be regarded as an expression of "The General Will". And although he thought that in principle the State should own everything, in practice he agreed that individuals should be allowed to own property, and accepted that economic inequalities were inevitable. He did, however, insist that there should be no extremes of wealth and poverty, because that would lead to corruption in political affairs.

NO CITIZEN SHALL BE RICH ENOUGH TO BUY ANOTHER ONE, OR SO POOR AS TO BE OBLIGED TO SELL HIMSELF.

The Test Case of Corsica

Rousseau was not in favour of tearing down traditional societies to replace them with some theoretical totalitarian blueprint. In 1764, Buttafoco, a Corsican officer, asked Rousseau to provide the islanders with their own constitution. The political status of the island was precarious. Rousseau found out as much as he could about the island's history, geography, religion, social institutions, resources and existing laws.

THEY SHOULD CHOOSE A REPUBLICAN GOVERNMENT SIMILAR TO THE GENEVAN MODEL.

THE FIERCELY INDEPENDENT AND BRIGANDISH LOCALS SHOULD TRY TO DEVELOP A GREATER RESPECT FOR THE RULE OF LAW.

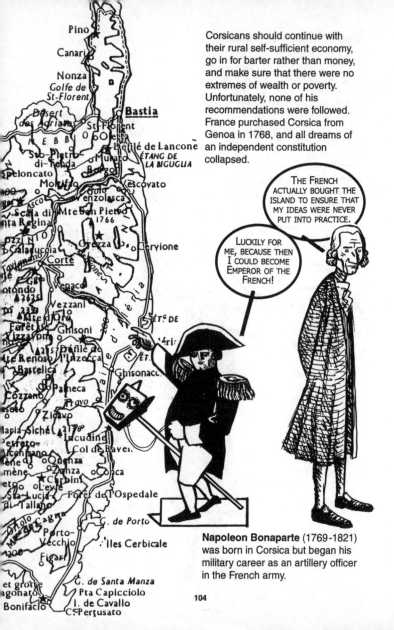

Corsicans should continue with their rural self-sufficient economy, go in for barter rather than money, and make sure that there were no extremes of wealth or poverty. Unfortunately, none of his recommendations were followed. France purchased Corsica from Genoa in 1768, and all dreams of an independent constitution collapsed.

THE FRENCH ACTUALLY BOUGHT THE ISLAND TO ENSURE THAT MY IDEAS WERE NEVER PUT INTO PRACTICE.

LUCKILY FOR ME, BECAUSE THEN I COULD BECOME EMPEROR OF THE FRENCH!

Napoleon Bonaparte (1769-1821) was born in Corsica but began his military career as an artillery officer in the French army.

The Test Case of Poland

In 1771, Rousseau also wrote **Considerations on the Polish Government** for Count Wielhorski. This time Rousseau suggested that the monarch should be electable, taxation made more equitable, education reformed, and that Poland should be more federal in its political constitution – that way the citizens got more say in how they were governed.

BUT POLAND WAS PARTITIONED IN 1772 AND SO MY IDEAS WERE NEVER REALIZED EITHER.

IN BOTH TEST CASES, I BELIEVED THAT POLITICAL CHANGE SHOULD EVOLVE GRADUALLY OUT OF EXISTING INSTITUTIONS, TRADITIONS AND LOCAL BELIEFS.

All of which seems to have made him more of a conservative than a revolutionary. Rousseau in practice was less radical than many of his zealous French revolutionary followers would have liked him to be.

Criticisms of Rousseau's Political Theories

There have always been fierce disagreements about the political writings of Rousseau. **The Social Contract** can be read in many different ways, which worries some scholars, but for others is another sign of his true greatness. Is Rousseau a benign liberal or a totalitarian monster?

Rousseau was not always a very logical or coherent thinker, but wrote very persuasively, and tends to say things like "forced to be free", which sounds very sinister but probably isn't. Let's begin with a critical look at Rousseau's "General Will".

"The General Will" Under Scrutiny

We have seen how important the mysterious entity of "The General Will" is to Rousseau's political philosophy. The phrase was current in French thought and used by writers like Diderot.

IT MEANS SOMETHING LIKE "THE PUBLIC INTEREST". BUT ROUSSEAU GIVES IT HIS OWN UNIQUE MEANING.

HIS RADICALLY DIFFERENT DEFINITION OF "SOVEREIGNTY" MARKS HIM OUT AS A NEW AND DISTINCT KIND OF POLITICAL THINKER.

EVEN IF MANY OF HIS IDEAS ACTUALLY CAME OUT OF ANCIENT GREECE.

"LIBERAL" PHILOSOPHERS LIKE HOBBES AND LOCKE THINK OF SOCIETY AS "ATOMISTIC" ...

LITTLE MORE THAN JUST A COLLECTION OF DIFFERENT INDIVIDUALS.

BUT I REALIZED THAT, ALTHOUGH INDIVIDUALS MAKE UP A SOCIETY, THEY ARE NOT ITS WHOLE.

For the collectivist Rousseau, "society" is a metaphysical entity with its own separate existence. And just as an individual can have a "will", so society can have its own will – "The General Will" – and this is something more than just the sum of all the wills of its individual members or "the Will of All".

A Nebulous Concept

But when you examine what Rousseau says more closely, it's increasingly hard to see how "The General Will" really exists or in what form. Individuals clearly have bodies, feelings and desires, but "The General Will" doesn't have that kind of existence. It's a very abstract and mystical kind of entity. That may not mean that it doesn't exist at all.

PHILOSOPHERS ARE VERY AWARE OF ENTITIES LIKE "GRAVITY" AND "MINDS" WHICH ARE EQUALLY HARD TO DEFINE INTO SOME KIND OF THIN "EXISTENCE".

SOCIOLOGISTS ALSO BELIEVE THAT "SOCIETIES" EXIST, OVER AND ABOVE THEIR INDIVIDUAL MEMBERS, OR THEY'D BE OUT OF A JOB.

NEVERTHELESS, THERE PROBABLY ISN'T SUCH A THING AS "THE GENERAL WILL" REALLY.

And even if there is, it would probably never be the pure and infallible moral guide Rousseau wanted it to be.

Rousseau thought that his "upright and simple people would be hard to deceive", but majority opinion is often all too easy to manipulate and can frequently be quite foolish or even harmful. Rousseau's perfectly moral "General Will" could only ever exist in an ideal state composed of ideal citizens. But in the real world neither exists, so there is no magical way of discovering what "The General Will" could be. How would you discover what it was and know that it wasn't just "The Will of All"?

MERELY BY UNANIMOUS OR MAJORITY AGREEMENT?

BY SOME KIND OF STATISTICAL AVERAGING PROCESS WHICH CANCELS OUT ALL THE "PLUSES" AND "MINUSES" OF DIFFERENT INTEREST GROUPS?

BY RELYING ON A SEMI-DIVINE LEGISLATOR?

IT'S A NEBULOUS CONCEPT ON WHICH TO BASE A WHOLE POLITICAL PHILOSOPHY.

The General Will and the Law

There will always be disagreements about moral issues like, say, euthanasia and abortion, so it's difficult to see how Rousseau's citizens could always arrive at a total consensus.

PEOPLE HAVE DIFFERENT TASTES AND VALUES.

SOME WANT FAST NEW ROADS.

OTHERS WANT UNSULLIED COUNTRYSIDE.

It's easy to see how a body of similarly minded people like a group of Quakers, or members of a coach tour, could easily draw up a code of conduct that members could vote on and then be expected to obey. But it's harder to see how every single citizen of even a small country could meet regularly and reach rapid agreements about the law.

A Romantic View of Communal Life

Rousseau wrote **The Social Contract** with the best of intentions. He was an outsider and an idealist who often found it difficult to cope with the civilized world. He had no experience of the everyday grubby world of political compromise. But he still had a profound longing to be a part of a community. In his novels, he rhapsodizes about the ritualized social life of small agricultural peasant communities.

I LOVED PARTICIPATING IN WEDDING PARTIES, GRAPE HARVEST FESTIVALS AND OTHER LOCAL OCCASIONS.

He recognized how, in such shared public events, every individual in the community has an important role to play which displays some aspect of loyalty to the community.

The Collectivist State

Rousseau had deeply romantic and quite reactionary views about the harmonious joys of traditional village life. He ignored or forgot about the often oppressive nature of small communities. His collectivist instincts may be sentimental and often naïve, but they're not particularly tyrannical.

BUT THERE ARE SOME PARTS OF **THE SOCIAL CONTRACT** THAT ARE PROFOUNDLY WORRYING.

HOSTILE CRITICS WHO ACCUSE ROUSSEAU'S POLITICAL PHILOSOPHY OF BEING POTENTIALLY "TOTALITARIAN" ARE NOT BEING WHOLLY UNFAIR.

Rousseau demands that everyone must surrender their individual rights to the very imprecise "General Will". But if there is no recognition of individual human rights, then, as recent experience has shown, the State will become much too powerful.

ROUSSEAU PLACES NO ADEQUATE CHECKS OR BALANCES ON THE SOVEREIGN AUTHORITY OF HIS COLLECTIVIST STATE.

He relies too much on the infallible goodness of citizen assemblies and semi-divine lawgivers, to ensure there is no oppression.

Public or Private Freedom?

Rousseau's society would be easy prey to some individual or group who claimed to be the living embodiment of "The General Will", and thereby suspend the citizens' legislative assembly and rule with a total disregard for all civil liberties. In 1814, Napoleon did precisely that. He announced to the Corps Legislatif that …

"Freedom" is a word that is impossible to define with any precision, although most of us have a rough and ready set of ideas about what it means when it comes to our own property, speech and religious beliefs. Rousseau couldn't imagine why his legislative assembly would ever pass laws that unnecessarily interfered with individual freedom.

BUT BY IGNORING PRIVATE FREEDOMS AND PLACING ALL THE EMPHASIS ON HIS **PUBLIC** "MORAL FREEDOM" ...

ROUSSEAU MAKES IT TOO EASY FOR THE STATE TO CLAIM A MONOPOLY ON PERFECTION AND TAKE TOTAL CONTROL OVER PEOPLE'S LIVES.

What Makes Good Citizens?

It seems to be in the very nature of governments to be hungry for absolute power. This is why modern democracies try to ensure that there are always some checks on governments in the form of things like an independent judiciary and a free press.

Rousseau's political vision can very easily be criticized as idealistic and naïve. To some extent it's based on his own distant childhood memories of a highly idealized Geneva Republic with its two "Councils". It's also grounded on his early adolescent readings of Plutarch and his admiration for ancient classical models of citizenship.

CLASSICAL PEOPLE WERE CLEARLY MORE COLLECTIVIST.

WHICH, FOR ME, IMPLIES THAT HUMAN NATURE IS HIGHLY MALLEABLE AND CAN ALWAYS BE CHANGED.

IT IS BETTER TO IMPROVE MEN THAN TRY TO DEAL WITH THEM AS THEY ARE.

Patriots or Hypocrites?

Rousseau wanted to create "new men" who were moulded from birth to be separate yet patriotic citizens, passing laws that were always in the collective interest. But, refusing to legitimize the existence of interest groups and political parties leads, not to a society of robust and independent individuals, but to the centralization of State power.

IT ALSO LEADS TO AN APPALLING KIND OF COMPULSORY HYPOCRISY.

EVERYONE MUST FABRICATE A PUBLIC AND VISIBLE LOYALTY TO THE STATE.

THOSE WHO SHOUT THE LOUDEST ARE USUALLY THOSE WHO HAVE THE MOST TO GAIN FROM SIMULATED PROTESTATIONS OF CIVIC DEVOTION.

The Persecution of Jean-Jacques Rousseau

Both **Émile** and **The Social Contract** were condemned as soon as they were published. Rousseau spent the last years of his life on the run, hiding out under an assumed name in different small provinces and on various French country estates. How much personal danger he was in is debatable, but the very real persecution of his work and ideas served only to reinforce his overpowering feelings of betrayal and injustice.

Geneva and Holland both banned **Émile**. In 1763, the Archbishop of Paris wrote a pamphlet accusing Rousseau of hypocrisy. Rousseau replied in yet another public "letter" which clarified his doctrine of man's original goodness and defended his beliefs in a "natural religion".

Rousseau Attacks Geneva

Rousseau then renounced his Genevan citizenship for the second time and, as a Stateless person, fled to Môtiers-Travers. Here he wrote yet more angry public "letters" to the intolerant Genevans who he thought were behaving like the Catholic Inquisition. (**Letters Written from the Mountain,** 1764.) In these letters he defended the central ideas of **Émile** and **The Social Contract**, and accused the Genevan Church of being intolerant and prejudiced.

THE ESSENCE OF PROTESTANTISM IS TOLERANCE. EVERY BELIEVER IS FREE TO INTERPRET THE GOSPELS ACCORDING TO HONESTLY HELD BELIEFS.

Temporary Safety

Rousseau's letters also made more specific attacks on the Genevan government. Rousseau thought that the Petit Council (the executive) had awarded itself too much arbitrary power at the expense of the General Council (the citizens' assembly). Eventually Rousseau found another rich patron – the eccentric Scottish exile, George Keith, the Governor of Neuchâtel.

HE AGREED TO DEFEND ME ...

PROVIDED YOU ABANDON ALL RELIGIOUS CONTROVERSY FORTHWITH.

On the Run

For a while, Rousseau resumed an idyllic existence. He made several excursions into the Jura mountains, pursuing his new interest in botany. He also began to write his **Confessions**. But his reputation soon caught up with him. The local villagers threw stones at his house.

Visitors

While there, Rousseau had many visitors, including the economist **Thomas Malthus** (1766-1834) and the young Scot **James Boswell** (1740-95), who later became famous as Samuel Johnson's biographer. Boswell teased the great man relentlessly, and recorded their several conversations. Rousseau seems to have enjoyed his company.

Exile to England

Boswell also claimed to have been seduced by Rousseau's companion, Thérèse.

But sadly there are also clear signs from Rousseau's correspondence of this time that he was becoming increasingly unbalanced. He was exhibiting many of the classic symptoms of paranoia. He saw plots everywhere, all of which were part of a huge pan-European conspiracy to attack him and his work. The intrigue involved all of his old friends, the *Philosophes*, the Catholic Church and anyone else that he had recently taken a dislike to. Friends offered him sanctuary in Strasbourg and the Ukraine, but he finally chose England.

Another Quarrel

The philosopher David Hume admired Rousseau's work and had offered him refuge. Rousseau left France, exiled himself first to London, then Chiswick, and then to Wootton Hall in Staffordshire. In London he met members of the royal family, and spent some happy days botanizing in the Thames valley, accompanied by his dog, Sultan. But a silly joke letter written by Horace Walpole, one of Hume's friends, which gently mocked Rousseau for his eccentricity, quickly convinced him that Hume was yet another traitor.

> IN FACT, I WAS ATTEMPTING TO GET ROUSSEAU A ROYAL PENSION.

> WHICH I AT FIRST REFUSED.

Hume wrote a **Concise Account** of this unnecessary quarrel. Rousseau eventually fled back to France, saying, *"Sir, I want to depart from England or from this life ..."*

Return of the Exile

In France, he stayed with the amiable **Mirabeau** (1749-91), who sensibly agreed with everything Rousseau said, however mad. Rousseau then retired to Prince de Conti's château at Trye for a year where he was plagued by yet more visions of dreadful persecution.

IN THE SPRING OF 1768, I RECOVERED SOMEWHAT AND LEFT FOR LYONS AND GRENOBLE, STOPPING OFF TO VISIT THE GRAVE OF MME DE WARENS.

HE NOW CALLED HIMSELF "M. RENOU", WHICH PROBABLY FOOLED ABSOLUTELY NOBODY.

It was at this time that he finally married Thérèse who, by now, had taken control over most of his life.

Back In Paris

Rousseau returned to Paris. He was famous. He received many visitors, played chess with friends and went to the opera. He also spent much of his time writing vehement letters to old friends, and being pestered by a female admirer called Marianne. In the last eight years of his life he spent his time copying music, botanizing around the countryside around Paris, making and selling collections of herbs, and finishing off his **Confessions**, on which he had been working for several years.

I ARRANGED TO GIVE PUBLIC READINGS OF THE **CONFESSIONS**, WHICH ALARMED MANY OF MY OLD ENEMIES.

Mme d'Épinay, with much help from Voltaire, wrote some libellous memoirs as a reply, as did both Grimm and Diderot.

The Confessions

The **Confessions** were written over a period of several years. Rousseau's motives for writing them also changed. In 1764, he read Voltaire's vitriolic **Sentiments of the Citizens**.

Rousseau's **Confessions** opens with these defiant words ...

The Need for Confession

The **Confessions** is a remarkable work. It certainly shocked many 18th-century readers accustomed to the understated delicacy of **La Nouvelle Héloïse**. Rousseau is often explicit about his sexual feelings and amorous encounters. He confessed to mild forms of exhibitionism, masochism and much sexual guilt. He was determined to make the language of his confessions immediate and "transparent" so they would convey the honest truth about his life directly. He also hoped to obliterate the false public image that many people had of the monstrous "Jean-Jacques".

I WOULD PREFER TO BE KNOWN AS I REALLY AM, WITH ALL MY FAULTS, RATHER THAN SOMEONE WITH IMAGINARY VIRTUES WHO IS NOT ME.

Nothing But the Truth

By confessing to everything, Rousseau also hoped to understand himself better, and come to terms with the man he now was. Confession helped to remove guilt.

THIS WEIGHT HAS THEREFORE REMAINED UNRELIEVED ON MY CONSCIENCE UNTIL THIS DAY AND I CAN SAY THAT THE DESIRE TO UNBURDEN MYSELF OF IT HAS PLAYED A GREAT PART IN MY DECISION TO WRITE MY CONFESSIONS.

Rousseau confessed to many misdeeds: worst of all, abandoning his five children to a foundling hospital. None of these disclosures ever deterred him from a vigorous defence of his actions. He insisted that his intentions were always without malice. Confession may make Rousseau a sinner but, in his eyes, it also transforms him into a strangely heroic figure. And the more honest his confessions are, the more his readers will think him reliable and so accept his attacks on others.

The factual details of the **Confessions** are accurate enough. Rousseau, like most of us, is mostly only self-deceived rather than being a deliberate liar. His recollection of events and time is subjective. When he is happy his memory extends time, and when he is miserable it contracts it. **Confessions** is also a very consciously constructed literary work.

Like a Novel

Rousseau presents his life to us as a pattern. He draws parallels between different characters and events, inserts letters and speeches into the narrative at crucial times, employs flashbacks, and anticipates events to give his life story a powerful narrative drive. **Confessions** is really a remarkable autobiographical novel – full of imagination, poetic eloquence and psychological intensity.

Psychological Insight

Rousseau believed that his **Confessions** was a deeply moral work. By reading a true and uncensored account of a life other than their own, readers would deepen their understanding of human nature, and be less willing to judge others. Rousseau is also convinced that all the clues to his personality lie in his past.

Rousseau can be self-obsessed, vain, hypocritical and vindictive at times, but what finally emerges from a reading of **Confessions** is the direct voice of a man always determined to be himself. Hume, who thought it impossible for anyone ever to tell the truth about themselves, disagreed. He thought that Rousseau had to be fooling himself.

The Meaning of Confessions

The **Confessions** is many things. It's partly a lament for times past; partly the story of a young man searching for a mother substitute; partly a search for that lost childhood that Rousseau always regretted leaving behind. He was mostly happy as a young child, and a wonderfully carefree and adventurous adolescent.

ON MY TRAVELS, I WAS BEFRIENDED BY INDIVIDUALS FROM ALL CLASSES OF SOCIETY, TRAMPS AND NOBILITY. ALSO RATHER INNOCENT, GENUINELY UNAWARE OF MY OWN SEXUAL ATTRACTIVENESS.

He idolized young aristocratic women who often reciprocated by giving him shelter (notably in the two "paradises" of Les Charmettes and The Hermitage). **Confessions** describes the beauty of these refuges and relives the joys of the simple and solitary life that he led. But rival lovers, "society" and intolerant institutions conspire to destroy him, and the idylls vanish.

Confessions and the "System"

Rousseau was an older and maybe wiser man in his 50s when he wrote about his earlier days, of the times when he was innocent and untainted by compromise and the betrayals of adult life. In **Confessions**, he shows us how his own life story illustrates the truths of his philosophical "system".

138

Rousseau's Dialogues

By 1772 Rousseau was increasingly paranoid and fearful of both real and imaginary persecutors. It was at this time that he began writing the extraordinary **Dialogues** in which he and "The Frenchman" hold a court-hearing on "Jean-Jacques", the infamously misanthropic author.

I ITEMIZE ALL THE CRITICISMS HEAPED AGAINST JEAN-JACQUES AND HIS WORK ...

WHICH "THE FRENCHMAN" HAS BEEN GULLIBLE ENOUGH TO BELIEVE.

AND THEN, I REFUTE THEM ONE BY ONE.

Dialogues isn't always a very illuminating read. It is often repetitious and shrill, and occasionally displays disturbing signs of almost pathological paranoia. In it, Rousseau also draws some rather absurd parallels between himself and Jesus Christ. *"I have always thought and still think of myself the best of men ..."*

"Who Is Not Against Me?"

In his deluded condition he thought that his manuscript would be stolen, so in February 1776 he decided to leave a copy to God's safekeeping by placing it on the altar of Nôtre-Dame cathedral.

This seemed to signal that even God was against him. So he wrote out a number of handbills entitled "To Everyone Who Still Loves Justice and Truth", and distributed them in the streets of Paris instead.

Dialogues isn't all ranting and raving. It also examines the differences between the public iconoclastic "Jean-Jacques" with his ferocious reputation, and the quieter and more private individual who just wanted to live a quiet and simple life.

Towards the end of his life, Rousseau was writing more private and introspective kinds of poetic prose works which concentrated on these personal feelings of loss. He was also inventing new kinds of artistic expression which allowed him to explore the mysteries of his imagination.

Reason, Imagination and Romanticism

Rousseau was in at the beginning of that complicated movement of ideas, values and new artistic modes of expression that now go under the label of "Romanticism". In the 18th century "Age of Reason", the imagination tended to be mocked as merely "fancy" and those who extolled its uses were dismissed as "feelers" or "enthusiasts". Rousseau always respected reason as a useful tool, but he knew that his imagination had always been the source of his original ideas. This is why he was interested in how the imagination functioned. He knew he had to be in a rather special state of mind to receive its wisdom.

IN REVERIE, ONE IS NOT ACTIVE, THE IMAGES TRACE THEMSELVES ON THE BRAIN AND THERE COMBINE, AS IN SLEEP, WITHOUT THE HELP OF THE WILL ...

Reveries of a Solitary Walker

Yet another sympathizer, the Marquis de Girardin, offered Rousseau refuge at Ermenonville, near Paris. Here Rousseau partially recovered his wits and spent the summer boating, playing chamber music, botanizing and telling stories to the Girardin children. He also started writing **Les Rêveries du Promeneur Solitaire**.

In this last book, he describes his hikes around Paris in some detail. He is always amazed and elated when he encounters different plants and wild animals that are new to him.

The Last Natural Man in Contemplation

Rousseau's excursions also have a more serious purpose. They allow him to commune with nature and with God. **Rêveries** still contains odd passages of shrill indignation and self-justification, but most of it is quieter, sadder and more agreeable. This time Rousseau was writing only for himself. By compiling a "shapeless diary" of his walks, he thought he would be able to store them up for his later years.

Rousseau began writing **Rêveries** in 1776 and they remained unfinished. They arose partly out of a sense of psychological devastation and other appalling feelings of self-doubt and betrayal. Increasingly Rousseau thought of himself as a disappearing species of "natural man", soon to be supplanted by a new materialist age of commerce and industry.

He now felt that his best work would remain unrecognized forever and that his ideas would never be vindicated. But he also knew that he could achieve moments of temporary tranquillity by turning in on himself and using his imagination to recapture past experiences. In **Rêveries** he reminisces about the intense happiness of his early life, and defends his peculiar habits of solitary walks and lengthy periods of introspection.

Rousseau always had to be in natural surroundings for these "reveries" to occur. Contemplation was more than just idle dreaming – it was the only way to find mental, emotional and spiritual contentment.

I CAN ACHIEVE SHORT PERIODS OF TRANQUILLITY AND HAPPINESS BY ALLOWING MY MIND TO WANDER INTO A STRANGE HYPNOTIC STATE AND SO FORGET PAINFUL THOUGHTS.

In Book Five, he describes the intense happiness he experienced when he was exiled on the Île de St Pierre. By entering a profound state of contemplation he had been able to lose all sense of time and achieve something close to spiritual ecstasy.

"When evening drew near I used to love to sit at the lakeside, on the shore, in some hidden sanctuary. There the sounds of the waves and the rippling of the water fixed the attention of my senses and purged my soul of all other agitation, plunging it into a delicious reverie ..."

BECAUSE THE NATURAL WORLD HAS A DIVINE ORIGIN, IT THEREFORE HAS THE POWER TO AFFECT THOSE WHO CONTEMPLATE IT.

When Rousseau examined it closely, nature revealed its true harmony and proportion to him, qualities which he realized could also be discovered in the human soul. He was finally able to see how he had a place in the universal scheme of things.

"A deep and sweet reverie seizes the senses and you lose yourself with a delicious drunkenness in the immensity of the beautiful system with which you identify yourself. I feel indescribable ecstasy, a melting delirium, when I identify myself with the whole of nature ..."

What is new and different about Rousseau's last work are the ways in which he powerfully dramatizes these subjective experiences, so that his readers are able to share them. Rousseau was often awkward in company and reluctant to discuss his ideas with others.

So, to some extent, the act of writing for Rousseau was often a form of **therapy** which finally allowed him to achieve a deeper understanding of his authentic self.

In the 1770s, towards the end of his life, Rousseau spent much of his time transcribing music in the mornings and searching for herbs in the countryside around Paris in the afternoons. He wrote several long letters on botanical matters to friends and colleagues throughout Europe. In May 1778, he complained of stomach pains and took to his bed. He asked for the window to be open so he could see the trees in the park.

SEE HOW PURE THE SKY IS, THERE IS NOT A SINGLE CLOUD. DON'T YOU SEE THAT ITS GATE IS OPEN FOR ME AND THAT GOD AWAITS ME?

The End

On 2 July, Rousseau tried to get out of bed, but fell on the floor and was afterwards found to be dead. He probably died of uraemia, although unsubstantiated rumours soon started that he had committed suicide. A death mask was taken of his face which still shows the mark on his forehead made by his fatal fall. He was buried on a small island in the park of Ermenonville.

Thérèse was determined that neither the **Confessions** nor the **Dialogues** should ever be published. She decided to marry Girardin's English valet, valet, John Bally, but she was transferred to Plessis-Belleville nearby to avoid a scandal. Although Girardin provided her with a generous pension, she always complained that he had stolen her husband's papers and cheated her. She was 80 years old when she died, 23 years later, in 1801.

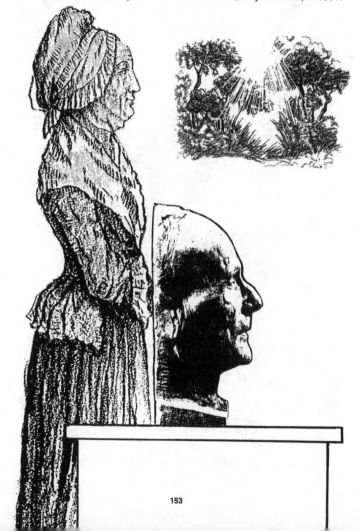

Rousseau the Many

Rousseau changed the world and the way people think. But can he be held responsible for all the claims made about him?

HE IS THE SOURCE OF THE FRENCH REVOLUTION AND THE REIGN OF TERROR.

HE IS THE FATHER OF ROMANTICISM.

... THE FOUNDER OF CHILD-CENTRED PROGRESSIVE EDUCATION.

EXISTENTIALISM CAN BE TRACED BACK TO HIM.

... THE FORERUNNER OF PSYCHOANALYSIS.

Is it possible to substantiate these claims? Let's examine them briefly, one by one.

The French Revolution

Eleven years after Rousseau's death, in 1789, the political life of France was totally changed by the Revolution. Rousseau's ideas undoubtedly stimulated revolutionary fervour in some of its leaders, although Rousseau himself would have been horrified by the wilful misinterpretations that were made of his words and the bloody excesses of the revolution itself. His remains were triumphantly transferred to the Pantheon in October 1794, although subsequently removed and scattered (together with those of Voltaire!) after the restoration of the Bourbons in 1814.

The Social Contract was little read when Rousseau was alive. But by the end of the 1780s it became immensely popular and had passionate radical disciples all over Europe. Rousseau was actually rather fearful of revolutions because he thought they normally had disastrous consequences. Nevertheless, his political works were adopted by both factions of the French Revolution – the moderate Girondists and the radical Jacobins.

FOR ALL OF US, **THE SOCIAL CONTRACT** BECAME A KIND OF REVOLUTIONARY BIBLE.

Intellectual radicals and more spontaneous *sans-culottes* demanded a new popular sovereignty and shouted boldly about "the will of the people".

The Reign of Terror

Instinctive authoritarians like **Maximilian Robespierre** (1758-94) and **Louis-Antoine St Just** (1767-94) referred to Rousseau constantly in their speeches and tried to establish a state religion – "The Cult of the Supreme Being". So, in some senses, Jacobin rule in the Reign of Terror (1793-94) was an attempt to make Rousseau's theoretical state a reality. Robespierre certainly thought of himself as the personal embodiment of "The General Will" and rather too willingly agreed with Rousseau's statement.

Other Followers of Rousseau

Since then, different generations of philosophers have interpreted Rousseau in their own ways, for their own purposes.

ROUSSEAU ENCOURAGED ME TO THINK OF MORALITY AS A UNIVERSAL CODE OF BEHAVIOUR WE MUST FREELY CHOOSE TO FOLLOW.

HE ALLOWED ME TO THINK OF THE STATE AS AN ABSOLUTE ENTITY WHICH SWALLOWED UP INDIVIDUALS IN A SERIES OF COMPLEX AND HISTORICAL DIALECTICAL PROCESSES.

I AGREED WITH ROUSSEAU THAT MEN ARE SELFISH BECAUSE A CAPITALIST SOCIETY MADE THEM THAT WAY. THE DAY MUST COME WHEN MEN ARE SOCIALIZED TO ACCEPT THAT SELF-INTEREST AND GENERAL WELFARE MUST COINCIDE.

ROUSSEAU'S VIEWS ON THE IMPORTANCE OF INDIVIDUAL FREE WILL, AND THE NECESSITY OF CHOOSING THE AUTHENTIC OVER THE SOCIAL SELF, LAID THE FOUNDATIONS OF EXISTENTIALIST PHILOSOPHIES.

IMMANUEL KANT

FRIEDRICH HEGEL

KARL MARX

JEAN-PAUL SARTRE

158

Postmodernism and Rousseau

Postmodernist philosophers like **Michel Foucault** (1926-84) certainly share Rousseau's belief in the plasticity of human beings, and are even more critical of social institutions whose primary function seems to be the conversion of free human beings into submissive "subjects". Rousseau was suspicious of the Enlightenment "project" from the start.

HE RECOGNIZED THAT POWERFUL INSTITUTIONS DETERMINE THE MEANING AND USE OF CONCEPTS LIKE THOSE OF "SCIENCE" AND "KNOWLEDGE" IN ORDER TO EXCLUDE AND DOMINATE.

SO, IN SOME SENSE, ROUSSEAU IS A VERY EARLY "POSTMODERNIST".

HOWEVER, MOST POSTMODERNISTS WOULD BE DEEPLY SUSPICIOUS OF THE COLLECTIVIST DOCTRINES THAT ARE VOICED IN **THE SOCIAL CONTRACT.**

MICHEL FOUCAULT

JACQUES DERRIDA

Perfect Citizens

Rousseau was an outsider who dreamed of a perfect society to which he could happily belong. But his ideal society is a regimented one in which very little free enquiry or discussion is allowed. It is suppressed in the name of "freedom".

Utopia or Dystopia?

Rousseau's fantasy of perfect citizens has aroused negative responses from writers of fiction as well as philosophers. Both **Aldous Huxley** (1894-1963) and **George Orwell** (1903-50) warned of the dangers of benign utopian fantasies that depend on forging "new men", because they very quickly turn into totalitarian "dystopian" nightmares.

The Totalitarian State

Rousseau was deeply committed to freedom for all, but unfortunately, not the kind of freedom that is preserved by different kinds of checks and balances on government power, or by human rights or by a pluralist society. He wanted people to be free from influential pressure groups and economic overlords, but never realized that the State could be an even harsher oppressor of individuals who have to live under its ever watchful eye.

I WOULD HAVE BEEN HORRIFIED BY THE INJUSTICES AND BARBARITIES COMMITTED BY 20TH-CENTURY TOTALITARIAN STATES AND OUTRAGED BY THOSE WHO WOULD MISUSE MY POLITICAL DOCTRINES TO DEFEND THEM.

He was probably neither a true collectivist nor liberal either, but a more complicated advocate of both. Nevertheless, nowadays, the political philosophy of **The Social Contract** has many fierce critics, partly because it seems to be an ambiguous text that is too easy to misappropriate.

Romanticism

Was Rousseau the "father of Romanticism"? The problem is defining Romanticism. We use it to name a phenomenon that began in the late 18th century and spread throughout Europe till the 1840s. It describes innovations in literature, art, music, philosophy and politics. Romanticism is seen as a "liberation" of the feelings from the rules of Classicism which prescribed "good taste".

A radical aesthetic was often matched by revolutionary fervour, a championing of individual or national rights against all forms of social and political oppression. Romantic themes are in appearance at least very like Rousseau's own – nature, children, love, imagination, rebellion against social norms and tyranny.

Rousseau, the Reluctant Romantic

Rousseau never claimed to be the founder of a new kind of sensibility. He used the word "romantic" merely to describe rocky landscapes (in **Rêveries**). He was never a conscious enemy of the classical artistic values of the Enlightenment. He still thought that "reason" was a valuable human asset.

WHEN IT IS USED TO COMPLEMENT THE WISDOM OF THE EMOTIONS.

And although, in his later works, Rousseau did write about "Romantic" themes like nature, the emotions, individualism and romantic love, his response to these things was varied and much less clear-cut than any kind of "Romanticism checklist" would suggest.

He was a scientific botanizer and a mystic, as well as an author whose writings on the natural world often possess intense visual power and startling clarity.

The Role of the Artist

Rousseau was often evasive and self-indulgent. He was vain, narcissistic and torn apart by simultaneous feelings of inferiority and superiority. He was a stateless outsider who never felt he really "belonged". But he did analyse the causes of his alienation.

Art for him was often a process of self-discovery. And it is this that probably makes him at least **one** of the true fathers of Romanticism. Rousseau's own character and the importance he gave it helped to transform the role of the artist and demonstrated the importance of the creative imagination.

Rousseau's Primitivism

Rousseau didn't invent the idea of "Primitivism" either, but he is probably its fiercest and most famous advocate. The Primitivist critique of civilization insists that we are miserable because we have abandoned a past golden age. We have made the bad mistake of choosing civilization and lost our "closeness to nature".

Nevertheless, Rousseau would still insist that civilization is bad for us, and perhaps he's right.

Ecological Prophecy

We modern civilized human beings aren't a very impressive or happy crowd. We are more addicted than ever to material wealth, produced by technological progress and the competitive efficiencies of the marketplace.

When Rousseau wrote his discourses, the world's population was small and the Industrial Revolution was just beginning. He couldn't have predicted that our modern "civilization" would also eventually make our planet uninhabitable.

The oceans are dying, the ozone layer is disappearing and the global climate is changing in ways that are catastrophically unpredictable.

The Costs of Civilization

Rousseau never claimed that civilization was all bad. It gives us writing, art, music, modern medicine, science, convenience foods, and books like this. But the cost of our modern civilization is clearly getting very high. He never suggested that we should turn back the clock. His "natural men" were, after all, just speculative fictions. But he did think that we should "get back on track".

Did Rousseau Have A "System"?

Rousseau never claimed to be a philosopher. *"I have never aspired to become a philosopher; I have never claimed to be one; I was not, am not, and do not, want to become one …"*

But he did have clear views about what human life was for. He believed that ideas could only ever be true if they were deeply felt to be so, even though the human condition was primarily one of ignorance.

*"We know neither our nature nor our active principle … impenetrable mysteries surround us on all sides … we think we have the intelligence to penetrate them, but we only have the **imagination** …"*

A System of Optimism

What emerged from Rousseau's own introspection was his "system" – a radical critique of Western civilization. What looked like progress was destruction and decline; social and political institutions were merely camouflage for economic and political exploitation.

But, although human beings had changed themselves into something awful, they could still return to something more "natural" and better. Rousseau had fervent and unique religious views which made him different from his contemporaries.

THE NATURAL WORLD - WHICH INCLUDES HUMAN BEINGS - CONTAINS A UNIVERSAL HARMONY AND MORAL ORDER IMPOSED BY GOD ON ALL REALITY.

THIS TRUTH HAS KEPT ME AN OPTIMIST.

Although men had lost sight of this truth, the potential for its rediscovery was always there in each individual, something that might one day lead to a harmonious society of virtuous citizens.

Paradoxes and Conclusion

Rousseau was a unusual man, full of paradox and contradictions. He was a sincere believer among sceptics, a prolific writer who condemned literature, a champion of individual freedom whose political doctrine is rigidly collectivist, a hermit who was desperate for approval, a progressive educationalist who packed his children off to an orphanage, a social rebel patronized by the rich, an intellectual who claimed that the natural man was happiest because he was free of ideas. He courted his readers and fled from their attentions. He was a sentimental dreamer, an impossible friend, and sometimes a vain and self-obsessed hypocrite. But he was, and always will be, interesting, precisely because of …

Further Reading

Rousseau was exceedingly prolific. He wrote novels, poems, essays, discourses, memoirs, reveries, confessions, dialogues, dictionaries, operas, plays, public and private letters, and various works on politics, anthropology, ethics, theology, war, psychology, aesthetics, botany and more. This means that not all of his work is easy to track down. His most important works are available as English translations.

The Social Contract and **Discourses**, translated and introduced by G.D.H. Cole, and revised by J.H. Brumfitt and J.C. Hall (Everyman paperback, 1983) is extremely useful and good value. The introduction is very informative.

Several of Rousseau's works are available in the Penguin Classics paperback series.

The Social Contract, translated and edited by Maurice Cranston (Penguin, 1970).
The Confessions of Jean-Jacques Rousseau, translated and introduced by J.M. Cohen (Penguin, 1954).
The Reveries of a Solitary Walker, translated and introduced by P. France (Penguin, 1979).

Many of the other major works are also available in other translations.

Émile, or On Education, translated and introduced by Allan Bloom (Basic Books, New York 1979).
Rousseau, Judge of Jean-Jacques: Dialogues, translated and introduced by J.R. Bush, C. Kelly and R.D. Masters (1990) and **Julie or La Nouvelle Héloïse**, translated and annotated by Phillip Stewart and Jean Vache (1997) are both in **The Collected Writings of Rousseau** (University Press of New England, New Hampshire) – the best source for those who wish to read all of Rousseau in English translation.
The Indispensable Rousseau, edited by John Hope Mason (Quartet Books, 1979) is also useful because of its wider selections from Rousseau's work.

Those fortunate enough to be able to read Rousseau in French can turn to the first four volumes of **Jean-Jacques Rousseau: Oeuvres Complètes**, edited by B. Gagnebin and M. Raymond (Gallimard, 1959).

There are many books about Rousseau, his life and his ideas.

Jean-Jacques Rousseau and his World, Sir Gavin de Beer (Thames and Hudson, 1972) is a useful introductory biography.
Rousseau, Robert Wokler (Past Masters, Oxford University Press 1995) is a clear and concise guide to Rousseau's ideas.

Jean-Jacques Rousseau: A Critical Study of his Life and Writings, F.C. Green (Cambridge, 1955) is a more thorough account of the man and his arguments.

The Philosophy of Rousseau, R. Grimsley (Oxford, 1973) is an extremely sympathetic exposition of Rousseau's complex thoughts and emotions. Others, like **Rousseau's Social Contract**, L.G. Crocker (Press of Case, Western Reserve University 1968) and **Jean-Jacques Rousseau and the "Well Ordered Society"**, M. Viroli (Cambridge, 1988) are more critical.

Rousseau: The Making of a Saint, J.H. Huizinga (London, 1973) is a rather ironic biography of the man and his ideas.

Those who wish to obtain a more thorough knowledge of political philosophy and so have a better idea of how Rousseau's work is often an ongoing debate with other thinkers could do no better than read both volumes of **Man and Society**, John Plamenatz (Longman, 1970).

This writer also found the following books extremely useful.

A Rousseau Dictionary, N.H.J. Dent (Blackwell, 1992).
Reappraisals of Rousseau (Manchester University Press, 1980)
– especially S.B. Taylor's essay "Rousseau's Romanticism".
The series **Critical Guides to French Texts**, Grant and Cutler, also contains some excellent guides to individual texts like **La Nouvelle Héloïse** (R.J. Howells), **Émile** (Peter Jimack), **Confessions** (Peter France) and **Rêveries** (David Williams).

Finally, those who think that the Rousseau of the first two discourses got it about right might like to read some more recent condemnations of civilization, and celebrations of "Neo-Primitivism" in **Against His-Story, Against Leviathan**, Fredy Perlman (Black and Red, Detroit 1983); **Elements of Refusal**, John Zerzan (Left Bank, Seattle 1988); and **Future Primitive** also by John Zerzan (Autonomedia, New York 1994). And if you prefer to exclude computers and the World Wide Web from the primitivist critique, you can download Zerzan's whole anthology of primitivist texts (**Against Civilization**) from
www.webcom.com/wildcat/home.html

Acknowledgements
The author would like to thank his long-suffering editor and occasional mentor, Richard Appignanesi, for making this book readable, as well as his colleague, the graphic artist Oscar Zarate, who helped to both clarify and enliven his text. He is also very grateful to his female companion, Judith, for more cups of coffee than are probably good for him, and the patient library staff of the University of Exeter, who managed to track down all the books by and on Rousseau that are mentioned above.

Index